A CHRISTIANITY WORTH BELIEVING

HOPE-FILLED, OPEN-ARMED, ALIVE-AND-WELL FAITH FOR THE LEFT OUT, LEFT BEHIND, AND LET DOWN IN US ALL

Doug Pagitt

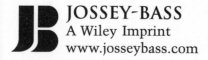

JOSSEY-BASS
A Wiley Imprint
www.josseybass.com

Published by Jossey-Bass
A Wiley Imprint
989 Market Street, San Francisco, CA 94103-1741—www.josseybass.com

Readers should be aware that Internet Web sites offered as citations and/or sources for further
information may have changed or disappeared between the time this was written and when it is read.

Jossey-Bass books and products are available through most bookstores. To contact Jossey-Bass
directly call our Customer Care Department within the U.S. at 800-956-7739, outside the U.S. at
317-572-3986, or fax 317-572-4002.

Jossey-Bass also publishes its books in a variety of electronic formats. Some content that appears in
print may not be available in electronic books.

Library of Congress Cataloging-in-Publication Data
Pagitt, Doug, date.
    A Christianity worth believing : hope-filled, open-armed, alive-and-well faith for the left out, left
behind, and let down in us all / Doug Pagitt.—1st ed.
        p.   cm.—(A living way : emergent visions series)
    Includes bibliographical references.
    ISBN 978-0-7879-9812-7 (cloth)
    1. Christianity—21st century.   2. Christian life.   3. Postmodernism–Religious aspects–Christi
anity.   4. Emerging church movement.   I. Title.
    BV121.3.P34 2008
    230—dc22

                                                                                    2008002654

Printed in the United States of America
FIRST EDITION
HB Printing   10 9 8 7 6 5 4 3 2 1

A LIVING WAY
emergent visions

CONTENTS

A LIVING WAY: EMERGENT VISIONS SERIES FOREWORD

I'm dubious of grand, historic-sounding proclamations, but when enough people say that we're in the midst of a spiritual reformation—even an old fashioned revival— it might be time to pay heed. Americans, and people around the world, are not becoming less religious; headlines make that clear. But we are becoming *differently* religious. We're thinking about God in new ways, and we're pioneering new ways to seek after God.

Of course, not all innovations in spirituality are salutary. Some strain the very fabric of the human community. Some tear it.

But others are beautiful and helpful and salubrious. It's these that we desire to publish.

For a decade now, a group of friends has been gathering under the banner, "Emergent Village." Officially, we describe ourselves as "a growing, generative friendship of missional Christian leaders." But amongst ourselves, we know that we're a band of spiritual renegades who have committed to live into the future *together*. We share life in profound ways, we care for one another, and we laugh a lot. I can't imagine a better group of friends.

And out of this cauldron of friendship and disillusion with religion-as-usual have come some ideas and some practices that have marked us indelibly. New ways of being Christian, of being spiritual, of following God have bubbled up in this group. We've tried, on occasion, to capture the magic before, like vapor, it slips away. That's not always easy, but sometimes it happens.

When our friends at Jossey-Bass approached us about capturing some of this magic in the pages of some books, it seemed like a great idea. It also seemed daunting. *Who are we to tell others how to live?* we wondered, *We're just figuring it all out ourselves.*

But it's become clear that it is the conversation that matters, not the conclusion; the journey, not the destination. Of course, this isn't a new thought in the history of spirituality— it's probably the oldest thought.

So, slowly and carefully, we enter into this realm, and we offer to you, dear reader, our humble attempts at what it means to follow God in this beautiful, worrisome age. We offer "A Living Way," for we firmly hold that God is alive and active in the world today; our job is to cooperate with what God is already doing. And we offer "Emergent Visions," because, even as we embrace them as our own in the here-and-now, we lean into the future, toward which God is beckoning us.

Doug Pagitt's theological memoir, *A Christianity Worth Believing*, fits the emergent phenomenon like a glove because it is a risky and hopeful theological endeavor. Doug is an adopted son in the Christian family, and his lack of Christian heritage gives him an unconventional set of eyes and leads him to some unconventional conclusions. He is not beholden to many of the theologies and practices on which many of us were weaned. In an era in which the cliché "thinking outside the box" is wildly overused, this book is just that. Doug considers himself a "hopeful, optimistic contrarian," and this important work charts his course to this point. It's sure to incite many of the very conversations that we in emergent so desire people to be having.

So, we welcome the conversation that we hope this book and others in the series will provoke. And we look forward to meeting you down the road so that we can have this conversation together.

Grace and peace to you.

Tony Jones
Series Editor

PREFACE

The other day my friend Brunsy asked me if I would like to have "one of the tastiest fruits I would ever eat." Of course I said yes, hoping for something ripe and sweet and perfect. So imagine my disappointment when he told me it was something called a plumcot. He explained that the plumcot is a cross between a plum and an apricot, a strange notion that didn't whet my appetite one bit.

I've never really understood this whole crossbreeding of fruit thing. I don't really get how they do it, and I really don't get *why* they do it. Are people so starved for new and exciting fruit that we demand genetic plant experiments? Anyway, Brunsy knows a thing or two about gardening, so I took a reluctant bite. It was fantastic. Who knew something so good could come from such an odd combination?

The plumcot isn't a bad metaphor for this book. The book is part memoir, part theological treatise—a tasty mixture of two writing styles. And honestly, I think all belief, all faith, is the result of a combination of experience, study, story, and understanding. My thoughts on Christianity are based in both what I've learned over the years and what I've experienced. So as you read, you'll find I move between odd little stories from my life and the bigger picture of Christian history. Not everyone will care for this mixture (although I can't imagine anyone not loving the plumcot), but I do hope it will be satisfying for those who are looking for a telling of the story of faith that comes from the reality of life.

The plumcot isn't just a nice way of talking about the structure of this book. It's also a great way of understanding the content. The plumcot suggests that we live in a world of possibility. Somewhere, somehow, someone imagined a new kind of fruit, a new flavor, a new color. Whoever fiddled with the plums and apricots was probably not trying to eradicate plums and apricots from the face of the earth but to offer something else, an alternative to what was already out there. I think that behind the plumcot is an intuition that life, even if it's just the life of produce, is never really settled. There is always room for a new idea, a new thought, a new fruit.

In the same way, this book is anything but a settled, secure, hard-and-fast understanding of faith that will work for all people for all time. It is not meant to provide the final answers to my questions about faith, nor is it meant to offer such once-and-for-all answers for its readers. Instead, it is my personal and often angst-ridden expression of a faith that feels alive, sustainable, and meaningful in our day. It is the outgrowth of decades of reading and studying and talking and experiencing and wondering and listening and engaging and arguing and rethinking.

It's not an overview of every theological idea that's come before, nor is it meant to be read as a stand-alone explanation of God and spirituality. It's not a "how-to-have-faith-like-me" sort of book. It is a "come-with-me-on-a-journey-of-exploring-the-possibilities" sort of book. And it is certainly not the end of that journey. There is so much more to say and learn about each of the topics in this book, and there are so many more topics on which to say so much more.

To me, faith is all about possibility. It's about the hope that we are made for something better than our often-limited human imagination might suggest. It's about the belief that we are part of God's great work in the world, that our hands and our minds, our very beings are tied to God in ways that surpass our understanding. It's about the vision of God's agenda coming alive right here, right now. And that's the faith I explore in this book. My hope is that as you enjoy this plumcot of faith, you will discover questions you didn't think you could ask, ideas you didn't think you could pursue, faith you didn't think you could hold on to. My hope is that you will discover a Christianity worth believing.

CONFESSIONS OF AN
ADOPTED SON

1

I am a Christian—a theologically trained, church-planting, evangelizing, Jesus-loving Christian. I trust in resurrection, and I seek to join with God in the world. But I have problem, an internal conflict that has only gotten worse in my twenty years of following this faith. It's the kind of problem I tell others about with great caution and no small amount of anxiety.

I am a Christian, but I don't believe in Christianity.

At least I don't believe in the versions of Christianity that have prevailed for the last fifteen hundred years, the ones that were perfectly suitable in their time and place but have little connection with this time and place. The ones that answer questions we no longer ask and fail to consider questions we can no longer ignore. The ones that don't mesh with

I am not conflicted because I struggle to believe. I am conflicted because I want to believe differently.

what we know about God and the world and our place in it. I want to be very clear: I am not conflicted because I struggle to believe. I am conflicted because I want to believe differently.

I don't like feeling at odds with the faith I hold so deeply. But I've come to believe these sorts of struggles are part of being adopted into a family that's been around for generations. And I know firsthand just how fraught with conflict the adoption process can be.

Seven years ago, my wife, Shelley, and I adopted our sons, Ruben and Chico. They joined our biological children,

Michon and Taylor, to make us a family of six. We quickly realized that the addition of these two did not just make us a third larger and a third Hispanic; it made us a new family. All six of us have hurt and grown and changed because of the shifting dynamics of our family. And I believe we are a better family with Ruben and Chico than we were without them.

Before becoming part of our family, Ruben and Chico were part of the foster care system and lived with our neighbors. Before that, they were living with their biological parents. Through adoption, their family and our family came together. That meant we had to learn one another's histories. We had to tell them our stories and listen to theirs. We couldn't force them to become Pagitts overnight but had to give them permission to be themselves. We have spent the last seven years figuring out how to embrace each other in order to be a new family.

There's a whole lot more to this process than simply adjusting to a different family system—setting boundaries, establishing authority, rethinking roles. There are endless ramifications to opening our family up to include the history, memories, patterns, habits, and assumptions of other people. Ruben and Chico, with their unique experiences, stories, pains, and passions, have changed who we are right now. But they have also changed who we will become. I sometimes wonder what it will be like if Ruben and Chico marry Mexican women and have children of their own who do the same. In a few generations, the name Pagitt will, for many people, be a Mexican name. These two children are now part of the Pagitt story, and they will forever alter the course that story takes.

As hard as adoption is for the adoptive family, it can be even more difficult for the adopted children. The first few months after Ruben and Chico became part of our family were particularly intense. Since we live next door to their foster home, the boys knew us fairly well before we adopted them, but moving in, making us their "forever family," was radically different from the occasional sleepover. This was the real deal. Our home wasn't a place to hang out but the place where they lived. They weren't visiting our family; they were re-creating our family. They still talk about how strange it was for them to look at us and realize we weren't the neighbors anymore, but Mom and Dad.

The boys have also told us that their most vivid memory of this odd transition is the collection of new smells. Every family has its own scent. Who knows how it comes about, but it seems to infuse the family's house, their clothes, even their skin. Naturally, smells that seem normal or even unnoticeable to the family are strong and distinct to others. Chico in particular says that when he came to our house knowing it would be his house, he noticed how different it smelled—and it scared him.

As adopted children, Ruben and Chico had a lot to learn: our smells, our rules, our customs, our humor. They were introduced to a new set of grandparents and friends. They had to make an unending series of adjustments. They brought their family pattern with them, but our structure was already set, and we had them outnumbered.

As Ruben and Chico began to find their way in our family, I thought about the ways their lives echoed my experience as a Christian. Growing up, I knew virtually nothing of Christianity or its characters. I didn't know Easter and Christmas had anything to do with each other, much less anything to do with the intricacies of religion. I grew up in a family of intentional nonchurchgoers. There was a church on nearly every corner that we didn't go to on purpose. I was never reprimanded for sleeping in on a Sunday morning, never taught how to look up verses in the Bible or sing songs to and about God. I never spent a summer at Bible camp or a week at vacation Bible school. The closest I ever came to setting foot in a church was when I was eleven and Danny Oakland and I broke into Good Shepherd Catholic School to steal playground balls and walked by the sanctuary on the way to the gym.

My family's deliberate lack of engagement with all things Christian was initiated by my dad. He never had much interest in religious life. His parents divorced in the 1930s, when divorce meant church ostracism. As a boy, my dad felt the pain of not being the "right kind of person for church." His bitterness at being turned away lasted the rest of his life.

My mom, on the other hand, was raised a tent-meeting Baptist convert, but my dad made her promise she would never force us to go to church. And she didn't. When it came to religion, my sister and I were on our own. It wasn't until my out-of-nowhere conversion at age sixteen that I paid any attention to things Christian.

I couldn't have asked for a warmer welcome to Christianity. I was embraced, discipled, and loved by wonderful people. As the adopted son in this faith family, I did my best to get used to the smells, memorize the names of the relatives, and follow the family rules. It was a wonderful beginning. I was asked to be part of it all, to bring my gifts and ideas and experiences to bear on the life of this family. Yet my gifts, ideas, and experiences have sometimes led me down roads that many in my family don't care to travel.

The thing is, I came into Christianity with a family pattern of my own, my own way of living and interacting, of processing and creating. My adopted sons are Mexican. I am a contrarian.

I have always seen the other side of an issue, a different perspective on the conversation. I am not a contrarian by choice; it's just part of me. I am pretty sure, even though I can't prove it (yet), that I am genetically predisposed to being "positively oppositional."

Just after my dad's death in 2001, the family of his second cousin contacted me to express sympathy. I had only a vague recollection of my father mentioning these people when I was a kid, but I figured it couldn't hurt to connect with this crew. So in 2005 we Minnesota Pagitts headed south to meet the Missouri contingent.

As wonderful as it was to connect with them, it was also incredibly strange. They kind of looked like me and even sounded a bit like me in spite of their slight Missouri twang. My kids, who'd never had cousins, were introduced to a whole family's worth of them. But the strangest moment was when my dad's cousin showed me some of the research he'd done on the Pagitt family. He handed me a placard with a short explanation of the origins of the family name. It traced our name back to 1623, and across the bottom it read, "The ancient family motto for this distinguished name was: *Per Il Suo Contrario.*"

I didn't need to know Italian to recognize the word *contrario*. I was stunned, to say the least. Could it be that my family, even back into the early 1600s, had been contrarians? That very real possibility felt like a confirmation that my contrarian nature was somehow built into me.

As soon as we got home, I got online and started searching for the meaning of this motto. Roughly translated, it means "Those who are contrarians" or "For it is contrary." People often think of contrarians as cynical, but I believe we are just the opposite. We are accused of playing the devil's advocate or of being provocative just for the sake of it. But to me, being a contrarian means holding out hope when others have stopped hoping. It means looking past the limitations and imagining the possibilities. It means rethinking ideas that have been ignored or dismissed in the past. I looked at that translation and knew that I wasn't just a contrarian, I was a contrarian carrying on the family heritage of wondering, questioning, and imagining.

These contrarian impulses don't always go over so well in my faith family. Religion, by its very nature, tends to be conservative. Not just in the political or theological sense, but in the truest sense of the word—to conserve something. Religion is often a tool for preserving a set of beliefs, ideas, and behaviors. That preservation necessitates a stance of protection, of warding off any change that threatens those beliefs.

The stickler is that Christianity doesn't make a very good religion in this sense. Christianity is not a faith of conservation and preservation. It is a faith of creation, participation, movement, and change. For conservation to happen, something needs to be stopped. Something needs to be limited. Something needs to be ignored. And too often that "something" is the unstoppable, unlimited, impossible-to-ignore activity of God at work in the world.

This is why things get tough for a Christian contrarian. Contrarians find life in hopeful possibilities. We tend to see what could be as so much more interesting than what has been.

It's natural for us to want to raise our hands after the final amen has been said. We are convinced that when we stop asking questions, when we turn away from a set of facts or an idea screaming to be considered, that's when things really fall apart. We are not trying to cause trouble; we're trying to stay out of it.

Like other families, established Christianity has particular ways of talking, eating, celebrating. It has history, memories, patterns, and assumptions that have set it on a certain course. And just as families have their crazy aunts that no one talks about, the church family has its "no-talk rules" to let everyone know what is and isn't open for discussion. It has set rules about who gets to talk and who gets to listen. Because of my personality, I crashed into these rules almost as soon as I became part of the family. I was like the kid who blurts out the family secrets at Grandma and Grandpa's fiftieth anniversary party.

Please don't misunderstand me here. I love my faith. I believe that living in the way of Jesus is the way humanity will embrace peace, justice, mercy, compassion, and love. I have seen my fellow Christians graciously, selflessly caring for the least among us. I have seen Christians who have found ways to live at peace with each other and in harmony with God. I have seen Christians following Jesus' command that we love others as we love ourselves, even when that love involves great sacrifice.

But while Christianity has given so much to the world, it too often carries with it a message, a belief system, that can be hard to believe. It too often creates a culture that is unintentionally hurtful to far too many people. I have a tendency to climb on my high horse of righteous opinion and make statements that imply (sometimes not very subtly) that Christianity is a stagnant, exclusive club for those who are satisfied with ill-fitting answers meant for issues of a different age. But when

I come to my senses, I'm convinced that if I'm ever going to feel like I truly belong to this family, if I'm going to live out the faith I profess in any kind of honest way, then I have a responsibility to break the no-talk rules and say what I believe the good news has been about all along. I am as responsible as anyone for the faith I profess. If I want to be a full participant in Christianity, I need to stop complaining about the beliefs articulated by others and make my contribution instead. In doing so, I am following the true legacy of this family.

For Christianity has always been a living faith, one presented in hundreds, even thousands of different ways around the world and throughout the ages. It has always been the dynamic interplay between the Spirit of God and the lives and cultures of people. It is meant to be a real-life journey of discovering, wondering, answering, and questioning.

> **Christianity has always been a living faith, one presented in hundreds, even thousands of different ways around the world and throughout the ages.**

This book is an articulation of that process. It is an expression of my desire for a Christianity that makes sense in the world in which we live, a Christianity that is not afraid of questions and will not resist answers, regardless of where they lead. It is my attempt to embrace a faith that is expansive, growing, and beautiful, one in which God is active and alive, involved in all of life. Because I believe in a Christianity where nothing is left out and no one is left behind, where humanity participates with God in the redemption of the world; where sin is more than a legal problem to be judged but a relational problem that can be healed; where we pursue harmony, centered on Jesus the Messiah, the Jew, whose life, death, and resurrection allow us to live well with God; where the Bible draws us into a story of life and healing; where we find hope for this life and life ever after; where love is alive, where love drives out fear, where love propels us toward lives lived for the betterment of all the world.

The Christian family will always include people who are satisfied with the way things are and people who want to see new possibilities come to life. And we are all better off because of the mix. No one should be removed from the family simply for wanting the benefits that come with conservation, and no one should be removed for wanting to move forward as the faithful have always done.

Toward that end, this book is a call, or a re-call, for those who believe the gospel of Jesus is an invitation for all people to live a dynamic faith as full members of the family, joining in the hopes, dreams, and aspirations of God for the world no matter what kind of family we come from.

2

PASSION PLAY

When I was growing up, my family had its own Sunday morning rituals: my dad played golf, and my sister and I watched TV while eating my mom's french toast triangles. (Decades before french toast sticks became a heart-stopping favorite on the Burger King menu, my mom had perfected the technique of frying batter-dipped Wonder Bread in the Fry Daddy.) In the winter, my sister and I had to eat quickly so we could make it to our bowling league on time.

This combination of TV, bowling, and deep-fried bread made Sunday mornings the second-best day of the week— second because nothing could outdo Saturdays with their promise of AWA Professional Wrestling. Most kids in Minnesota knew about Saturday morning wrestling on TV, but for the blessed few of us who lived in Golden Valley, just two miles from the Channel 9 studios, Saturday mornings meant hopping on our Huffy Thunder Roads to see Vern Gagne, Hulk Hogan, The Crusher, and the High Flyers in action and within spitting distance. Between the ringside seats and my mom's french toast triangles, my weekends were plenty full even without church. I had no idea other people spent their weekend mornings in their best clothes, sitting still, and eating tiny pieces of unleavened bread. It wasn't that I chose not to go to church. I didn't have church on my radar and never thought about it. I literally didn't know what I was missing.

Even though I had no Christian framework, I did have thoughts about and even faith in God. I'm not sure where this awareness of God came from, but it ran deep. I didn't know the story of God, yet I had a gut-level understanding that God was involved and active in the world and wanted people to join in that activity. I remember watching the movie *Billy Jack* as a twelve-year-old and thinking, *Now that's what God must be into.* Before I had any usable vision of Jesus, I saw Billy Jack as God's worker.

He was a half–Native American, half-Caucasian Vietnam vet with a black belt in karate, riding a motorcycle, living in the desert, and coming with fist and feet to the aid of native people who were being oppressed by "the man." Defending the powerless—and looking wicked cool doing it. Now there's a picture of God's agenda for the world that grabbed me. I wanted to be part of that agenda. I wanted to be the guy bringing justice, righting wrongs, protecting the weak.

> **I didn't know the story of God, yet I had a gut-level understanding that God was involved and active in the world and wanted people to join in that activity.**

The Billy Jack image of God hung in there and gave me some tangible picture of a possible life with God. But it also gave me the impression that God wasn't someone to mess with. So I made a deal with God: "If I don't hurt, kill, or rape anyone, then you won't utterly destroy me. OK?" I took God's silence as implicit agreement. My prayer wasn't very sophisticated, but it helped me feel like I was doing something to get my life in line with God.

This God was absolutely real for me. I had a big American flag hanging over the headboard of my bed. On those nights when I came home under the influence of some chemical, which was fairly common, I wouldn't let myself look at the flag. It just seemed unpatriotic and wrong. But

I would always pray my little prayer. I believed that God was near and approachable and didn't care what shape I was in.

Still, it wasn't enough. I knew that something wasn't quite right. There was a disconnect between who I was and who I wanted to be, but I couldn't figure out what it was or what to do about it. I sometimes wondered if it would have been better to not think about God at all than to know of God but feel so out of sync with God. I was lost. There was something out there, something I knew I wanted to find, but I couldn't even name what it was, much less make my way toward it.

In fourth grade, my buddy Charlie Lyons and I joined the Boy Scouts. Before the abrupt end to Troop 176 (brought on when our troop leader was charged with stealing the money we had raised through our Christmas wreath sale), we would take weekend trips during which we were taught to navigate our way through the forest, look for and leave clues, and use a compass and the stars as guides to keep us from getting lost. I never could figure out what we were doing in the woods. Not being much of a camper, I figured that the best way to not get lost in the woods was to stay out of them in the first place. Still, we scouts, even though we lived in urban Minneapolis, apparently needed to know these survival skills. So I earned my merit badges and learned all the tricks to track my way through the trees.

Life-tracking skills were another story. I didn't have a compass for life. I didn't have the tools I needed to trek through the forest of my confusion and fear. What I did have was the potential and ability to not just get lost but to stay lost.

I wasn't the only one wandering in this particular forest. Steve and I were best friends growing up, and he was equally unversed in Christianity. We lived in the Village Terrace apartments and shared the kind of unsupervised, we-run-the-show childhood that seems to be the birthright of apartment complex kids. Steve had a really hard go of it. His mom left the family when he was five, and his dad was hooked into all sorts of addictions. When we were thirteen, Steve was forcibly removed from his dad's care and placed in a foster home. Two years later, when Steve moved back in with his dad, it was clear to all of us at the Village that he had been "born again."

Steve carried a big Bible everywhere he went and talked constantly about Jesus. Steve's Jesus talk didn't make much sense to me. (My knowledge of Jesus started and stopped with John Lennon talking about being crucified like Jesus in "The Ballad of John and Yoko" and Bobby Bare's song "Drop Kick Me Jesus Through the Goalposts of Life.") But even I could tell that Steve, who had been the craziest kid I knew, had changed. Instead of being up for whatever destructive plan the rest of the apartment kids came up with, Steve was the guy hanging out his apartment window, yelling at us to stop doing whatever sinful thing it was we were about to do.

The spring of my junior year in high school, Steve asked me if I wanted to go with him to something called "The Passion Play." I thought the old Steve had returned. I mean, when a sixteen-year-old guy hears there's a play about passion going on downtown, well, let's just say I wasn't expecting it to be about Jesus. I agreed to go, and on Friday night, April 1, 1983, we hopped in my car, cranked up the John Lennon, and headed downtown.

We settled into the front row of the balcony of an old theater that had been turned into a church. The place had a strange smell to it—it smelled like old paper, old clothes, old people. The worn velvet seat creaked as I peered over the balcony railing to the stage below. As people filed into the rows of seats on the main floor, I sensed the excitement building in theater. It all felt so foreign to me. I had no idea what it was all about, and yet I couldn't wait to see what might happen.

The lights went down and the play started. As I watched the scenes from Jesus' life, I had this kind of déjà vu moment: I knew this story. The events themselves were new to me, but they had a strange familiarity to them—the kindness of Jesus, the loneliness of seeming abandonment, God standing with the weak.

As I watched the scenes from Jesus' life, I had this kind of déjà vu moment: I knew this story.

Then they got to the resurrection. Now there was a twist I didn't see coming. I had no idea something could trump the unbelievable and startling "Father forgive them" line Jesus screamed from the cross. But then Jesus came back and something inside me burst open with hope.

This was what I had longed for, what I'd needed to be true. There was God alongside the tortured and beaten Jesus. There was God on the side of people, bringing about goodness even in the midst of horror, betrayal, and struggle. There was God inviting people to join in the redemption of it all. There was God outdoing my vigilante, Billy Jack faith with something far better.

Sitting in my creaky seat, leaning over the railing, I felt my soul wake up. This was the story that was deeply planted in me. This was the completion of the story of God that had been in me from childhood. It was a bright, clear marker that

I knew could set me on a path toward . . . something. I sat in that smelly theater, surrounded by strangers, and knew I was home.

At the end of the production (which in a sort of cheesy but endearing way included Jesus flying up to the rafters for the ascension and then just hanging out on the catwalk), a man took the stage and starting talking. I wasn't listening to him; I was too distracted by what was happening inside me. I clicked into his instructions just as he invited those who were interested in learning more about this story to come backstage. I made eye contact with Steve, and he got up and started walking with me. As we moved toward the stage, I told God, *If this is truly your story, I will give myself to it for the next three months,* which seemed like plenty of time—I mean, that was all the way into summer! In many ways that awkward little prayer on April Fool's Day marked the beginning of my Christianity.

I had every intention of making the story I had just seen the navigational system of my life. I was going to live the Jesus way. I didn't know what that would mean, but I knew that whatever had just happened to me, it would change everything.

3

FROM AMEN TO UH-OH

Mark Twain once said, "It ain't what you don't know that gets you into trouble. It's what you know for sure that just ain't so."

Running into those things that "just ain't so" is something I have come to call an "uh-oh" moment. It's that time when reality opens up in front of you and you can either step into it or run away from it. That night at the Passion Play, I hit the first of my many spiritual uh-ohs, and I jumped into it with everything I had.

We all have our uh-oh moments: you find a lump that wasn't there before, and life changes in an instant; someone says "I love you" or "I don't love you," and the future takes on a different trajectory. When the uh-oh is fun and friendly—oh, you didn't know your aunt left you her entire fortune?—we embrace it. But those uh-oh moments that threaten our well-balanced life—oh, you didn't know your dad was once a jailed criminal?—well, those are the ones we'd rather avoid.

We might try all kinds of tricks to send them away: isolation, attack, marginalization, denial. But these work about as well as a teacher putting a talkative kid in the corner of the room in the hope the other kids will ignore her. She will not be quiet, and the other kids find her so intriguing, they head over to her and start up a conversation. Before long, this thing we hope to ignore not only keeps piping up but drags all our other supposedly solid beliefs down with it. These uh-oh moments can be dangerous things.

I have had uh-ohs in every aspect of my life—in job situations, in family dynamics, in friendships, in my understanding of who I am. But the ones that have really taken me aback are those that mess with my understanding of God and the

Christian faith. They are the ones that rip into all my other carefully tended assumptions. They are the ones that leave me reeling for years at a time.

It's ironic that faith and the uh-oh are so often turned into enemies. The disciples, who had witnessed Jesus performing miracles, didn't believe in the resurrection because it just couldn't be so. Galileo was forced to recant his belief that the earth was not the center of the universe because it ran against the church's official version of the "truth." The kid in Sunday school asks the wrong kind of question and is scolded for her doubts. The woman feels she can't tell her Bible study group about the benefits of her yoga class for fear of being labeled "new age."

The irony is that we religious people give tremendous importance to the uh-ohs that lead to initial conversions. We find these unsettling realizations so astonishing that we create testimonies relating the uh-oh moments in which we realized we needed faith. These conversions are celebrated and shared and held up as great moments in the Christian story. But once that initial shift has been made, our religious system holds little room for further uh-ohs, those that might challenge rules of the faith, even if they might move us toward a richer, more sustainable understanding of God. And that's unfortunate. Being once-and-for-all conversionists squelches the dynamics that created faith in the first place.

In some ways mine is the classic story of a dramatic, once-and-for-all conversion. Told in the right way, my conversion is a perfect example of "Amazing Grace": I was lost but now I'm found, I was blind but now I see. I was a captain of the high school basketball team, a recreational (and just a bit more) alcohol and drug user, a totally nonchurched, angst-ridden teenager—and now I'm the model of a fired-up, can't-wait-to-tell-my-friends Christian.

My faith uh-oh was so profound that I didn't just change; I changed with a capital C. During the first year and a half of my Christian faith, I helped start after-school groups for students interested in Christianity. I led Bible studies. I evangelized at my school and was suspended for distributing a religious newspaper. I was the lead litigant in a federal lawsuit against the school district for the violation of my constitutional right to freedom of speech and freedom of religion. As a result, I became a presenter at youth groups, churches, fundraising events, and conferences. I went to a Christian college, graduated from seminary, and became a youth pastor at a well-known megachurch where I helped reach other struggling kids. It was the kind of turnaround conversion youth group legends are made of.

While this is my "official" conversion story, one I have told many times, it is not the entire story. As in all stories, the details matter. To tell my story honestly, I need to include not only the conformity but also the wondering, searching, and reconstructing—the uh-ohs that were there from the start of my Christian life.

To tell my story honestly, I need to include not only the conformity but also the wondering, searching, and reconstructing—the uh-ohs that were there from the start of my Christian life.

Watching the Passion Play and discovering the story I wanted to live in was my first spiritual uh-oh. And it was a beauty. As I walked backstage, I felt like I knew what I was stepping into. I knew that God had a story, and I knew that God had a place in it for me. Yet within moments, my confident, hopeful faith was met with a second uh-oh, the kind that's not so pleasant.

I didn't mean to start my Christian life disagreeing with the powers that be. Really, I didn't. But in my heart I knew that what happened next simply didn't jibe with what I'd experienced mere moments before.

Steve and I sat in a circle with a dozen or so other people. There was a man there who told us he wanted to explain a few more things about the play we'd watched. He pulled out a bunch of little booklets, handed one to each of us, and started reading out loud as we followed along. From the first page I knew something wasn't right. I found it hard to accept that the wondrous story of God, the one I had just seen and been changed by, could be boiled down to bullet points and placed in a booklet. I wondered what happened to the version I'd just witnessed.

He finished the booklet and led us through a prayer meant to turn us into Christians. Even though I prayed the words, that prayer didn't mean nearly as much to me as the one I had improvised in the theater. I know this tract was meant to help new converts get the gist of the story of Jesus, but the booklet version made the story seem far more complicated than the joyous telling that had led me backstage. In fact, it made it seem like a different story altogether, one with steps and stages rather than people and passions.

My struggle with this version of Christianity increased ten days later when Steve and I met with two youth workers who graciously offered to "disciple" me—a term that sounded as odd to me the first time I heard it as it does today. Steve and I joined Bill and Kevin in a booth at the Burger King near my high school. As we dipped our fries in our chocolate shakes, I waited for Bill and Kevin to tell me that the play was everything I'd thought it was and that the life of God that had been growing in me over the last week and a half was a great start. But that wasn't how the conversation went. Instead, Bill turned over his placemat and wrote out what he called the "most important things" about Christianity.

This proved to be an even more disconcerting version of Christianity than the one I'd heard backstage at the Passion Play. In fact, the content of this conversation has caused me trouble to this day. (Even though I struggled with the explanation I recall Bill and Kevin giving me and know my memory of it may not fully convey what they intended, I am confident that it was the way they loved, protected, and modeled faith for me that kept me in the faith in the early years.) You can see what Bill wrote on the placemat—That's it, right there on the next page, a copy of the actual placemat. Take a look at the top. There it is in gray and white: "Truth = absolute." Bill then jotted down two phrases that have haunted me for decades: "3 essentials to salvation" and "3 assurances of salvation."

Think about those words: *absolute, essential, assurance.* These are the perfect words for once-and-for-all conversions, but they don't do much for the continual growth of an uh-oh faith. I had jumped into Christianity without any sense of the absolutes, without knowing the essentials, without a shred of assurance. I was taking a chance that this was the right story, and I trusted that it was. But could I prove it? Did

Transferable = "to pass on"
Truth = absolute.

#1   How To Be Sure you are a Christian

Soul   3 essentials to Salvation

1. Mind - intellect   1. Facts - christ Died
                                        "   Buried (I Cor. 15:3,4)
                                        "   aRose

2. Feelings - Emotions   2. Faith - A. Believing that Gio will Do
                              (Heb 11:6)   as He has promised
                              Eph 2 8,9   b Transferring your Trust

3. Will - Decider   3 Repent   To Turn 180°
                                                    (2 Cor 5:17)

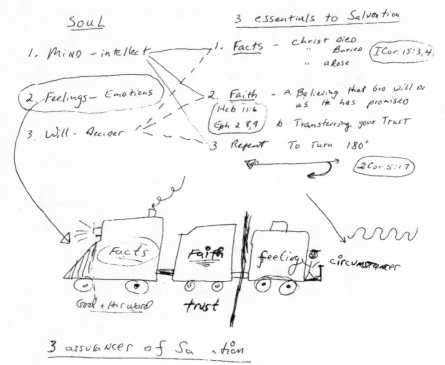

Facts   Faith   feeling   circumstances
God + His word   trust

3 assurances of Salvation

1) God and His the word   1 John 5:11-13

2) Witness of the Holy Spirit Romans 8:14-17   april 11, 1983
                                                   Stilton J Myers
                                                   Kevin J Young
3) Changed Life - II cor 5:17   Steven J Towley

I get it? Was I certain? No, no, and no. And yet my faith felt as alive then as it ever has. I was in the thick of something true, something meaningful. Even though I only had ten days of Christianity under my belt, those words crashed into my faith experience with a fury.

Next came the train cars. It was explained that the front car was the engine and the middle car was the coal car. The last car was the caboose. (This explanation was helpful as it was 1983 and I had never ridden in a train.) The cars were labeled: the engine was "Facts," the coal car was "Faith," and the caboose was "Feelings." Whatever they were actually saying, in my mind I heard, "The train needs only the first two cars— Facts and Faith—and can run just fine without Feelings." There was a hard line between the Faith car and the Feelings car (you can see it right there), as if, "Feelings and circumstances will change. You don't need them, and you can't trust them."

Now think about that. What is the point of a Christianity that doesn't involve our circumstances? The Bible is full of stories that are about faith lived out in particular circumstances. I got into Christianity because I *wanted* it to interfere with my circumstances. They have *everything* to do with faith.

I looked at the picture and realized that my train was running in reverse. I had experienced something real at the Passion Play and in the intervening ten days. I was in the midst of catching up on the facts and faith. If it was true, as the placemat said, that my faith had to start with my knowledge and the trust I had in that knowledge, then I had no faith at all because I barely knew a thing.

In spite of being unsettled by the explanation I recall hearing, I know Bill and Kevin were sincere in their effort to help me understand Christianity, so once Bill finished talking,

I folded up the placemat and put it in my wallet. It stayed there for fifteen years. Not long ago I scanned it into my computer and laminated it. I have often wondered why I kept it. I think it might have something to do with wanting to trace my Christian roots to someone or something. After all, next to the tract at the Passion Play, this was the first sermon, Sunday school lesson, or Christian teaching I ever heard. It has served as a reminder of the version of faith I was taught, the version I was welcomed into, struggled with for a long time, and gradually had to leave behind in search of something more hopeful.

I have been a pastor for a long time, and I understand the kinds of concerns that lead to the train explanation of faith. Some high school kid watches a play and thinks he's heard from God. It's not the most trustworthy scenario. Bill and Kevin wanted to be sure I didn't become discouraged when my life didn't change dramatically. They didn't want me to give up on my new, fragile faith. But the presentation provided a solution for a problem that wasn't there. My life had changed more than I thought it could, and I was anything but frustrated. I was more hope-filled than I had ever been in my life. I needed facts and faith to go *with* my feelings, not to replace or supersede them. Rather than starting with my lived experience and suggesting that there were other components I ought to consider adding—which I was desperately hungry for, by the way—the explanation for what had happened to me was a generic equation created years before.

I'm sure this version of the faith made sense to the people who first designed it back in the 1950s. They may well have had righteous reasons for choosing the "most important things" that applied to all people. But it did nothing to build my faith—quite the opposite: it sent me into a crisis. It's ironic that this attempt to keep me from feeling discouraged with my faith did exactly that—made me struggle. It's like getting sick from a vaccine. But what was I, a sixteen-year-old kid, suppose to do when long-term, faithful Christians were telling me the official story of the faith, even if it didn't match my experience? Question my experience, that's what. As often happens when hit by an uh-oh, I had two choices: either give in or give it all up right from the start, and I wasn't about to do that.

I have struggled with this version of Christianity from the beginning, but I have never wanted to give up my faith. I have always believed there could be a way forward that followed the story I was invited into, a story of hopefulness, of God's continuing presence in all our circumstances, a story with a call to live in the rhythm of God.

The issue here is not just the content of the placemat but the approach of making general requirements for all people. I believe that there is a way of living and telling the Christian story that connects with the **I believe that there is a way of living and telling the Christian story that connects with the life and experience of the person living it.** life and experience of the person living it. And I believe the only way to find that version of the story is to peel away the centuries-old veneer that covers Christianity, recognize the faith found there, and move forward with it embedded in our lives.

THE WILD GOOSE CHASE

4

I was a Christian for longer than I care to admit before I realized that the rainbow-haired guy in the end zone with John 3:16 written on his chest was pointing fans to a Bible verse—it takes some time for those of us not acquainted with Bible code to crack the obscure use of Bible references at football games. And it was years before I started to notice that the Bible wasn't a generic, objective history book, as so many people I knew had implied. The more I read it, the more I realized that the Bible was written to particular people in particular circumstances. It was shocking at first and increasingly good news as I realized that there was more than one version of the story of Jesus.

The placemat taught me that truth was absolute—not relative, not contextual, not experiential, but settled and unshakable. And I gave that approach my all for a good number of years. Yet there I was in seminary, studying the Gospel of John, when it occurred to me that John seemed to have a very different understanding of the "truth" than his fellow gospel writers. I noticed that there was no Christmas story in John's telling—no angels, no pregnant virgins, no doubtful husbands, no wise men. *Who puts together a biography of Jesus and leaves that stuff out?* I wondered.

Not only were there missing stories, but there were other stories that appeared only in John's telling. How could the other disciples leave out the resurrection of Lazarus, the water changing into wine, the healing of the man born blind? Even the stories John had in common with the other gospels were in a different order. I sat there staring at my Bible thinking, *Can he do that?*

I started asking questions, reading commentaries, and following the hermeneutical rabbit trails. What I learned is that John was telling the story in a way that made sense to his audience, so he made right and helpful adjustments to what he included and the order in which he placed his stories. By John's own admission, "Jesus performed many other signs in the presence of his disciples, which are not recorded in this book. But these are written that you may believe that Jesus is the Messiah, the Son of God, and that by believing you may have life in his name."[1]

John was telling the story of Jesus in a particular way so that the story would make sense to a particular group of people living in a particular culture—he was an evangelist, not a journalist. Many in John's audience were Greeks who would have held to the pervasive cultural belief that there were nine gods who ruled the world. John set out to show that Jesus was the fulfillment of all nine of these gods in order of importance. He arranged and built the story of Jesus to connect with his readers.

This is a crucial aspect of good communication and good storytelling, and it is a crucial aspect of the gospel itself. Though this makes sense to me now, it was totally revolutionary when I first considered it: The gospels are not generic, abstract truths. They are embedded stories. They are filled with culturally relevant language, images, and symbols that made them ring true in the hearts of their listeners. What is true for the gospel writers is true for us: the gospel is to be told in a way that makes sense in our day and time so that we too can find life in it.

I've noticed that people get nervous when I say things about contextual Christianity. I wonder if they're afraid that allowing the gospel to be contextualized turns the whole thing into a game of telephone, with one generation passing on its version of the story, only to have it misheard and miscommunicated by the next generation. Maybe they worry that the essentials will be lost over time and we will one day be left with a distorted, watered-down story that bears no resemblance to the one with which we started. But I think we have the opposite problem. The issue Christianity faces today is not that the stories are watered down; it's that they've been set in stone—often leading to the very distortion we fear.

When I talk about contextualization, I'm not talking about using pop culture connections to make faith more fashionable for the masses. I'm not talking about telling the same story with updated language. I'm talking about doing what John did—developing an intimate understanding of both our context and the story itself so that we can live faithfully in our day.

The earliest Christians were very good at this; every book in the New Testament bears the marks of contextualization—from the names of the people listed in the letters to the details of how to live faith in certain cities: Rome, Corinth, Philippi, Ephesus. Christianity has always been the hope of God through Jesus played out in the lives of real people living in real circumstances. Christians have never seen

Christianity has always been the hope of God through Jesus played out in the lives of real people living in real circumstances.

faithfulness as simply repeating a mantra. We have always been people of a living and active faith. It seems to me that it is a faithful practice for the church to continue those first-century efforts at telling the story in a way that makes sense to the people who hear it and live it.

This isn't a particularly radical idea. Whenever we tell a story—any story—we put it into a certain form, a culturally bound form with its own language and assumptions. This is not a choice we make, to either encode the story in culture or not. Encoding is a given. The choices we make involve choosing which cultural codes to use and recognizing when we have used them.

Metaphors like the train image I was shown back at the Burger King are meant to give us a clearer picture of Christianity. Metaphors, however, assume certain cultural norms. They assume that the person being shown the train diagram actually knows what a train is and how it works. This is probably not all that useful when explaining Christianity to, say, a primitive tribe in the jungles of Brazil. That's why missionaries spend a great deal of time trying to find culturally significant metaphors when speaking with people in other parts of the world. They recognize that the way they tell the Christian story may make sense in one situation but not in another. They know that faith is not universal but in fact very particular.

For example, missionaries working with the Masai people in Kenya and Tanzania created a creed that would make sense for that culture. This beautiful and useful statement includes phrases from the Masai culture: tribes, village, safari, and even hyenas.

We believe in the one High God, who out of love created the beautiful world and everything good in it.

He created man and wanted man to be happy in the world. God loves the world and every nation and tribe on the earth. . . . We believe that God made good his promise by sending his son, Jesus Christ, a man in the flesh, a Jew by tribe, born poor in a little village, who left his home and was always on safari doing good, curing people by the power of God, teaching about God and man, showing that the meaning of religion is love. He was rejected by his people, tortured and nailed hands and feet to a cross, and died. He was buried in the grave, but the hyenas did not touch him, and on the third day, he rose from that grave.[2]

This is not just an issue of what words to use. Language not only represents understanding but creates it. When we change the words, we change the story. Take, for example, the story of my goose.

There's a ten-foot-long papier-mâché goose hanging in our church. It might not be the first thing you notice when you walk into the room, but once you see it, you can't take your eyes off of it.

The goose arrived at the hands of an HIV-positive nomad artist named Michael who contributed to an art event we were putting together for Pentecost Sunday. Several of the artists at our church decided that it would be interesting to tell the story of the coming of the Holy Spirit at Pentecost through dance, drama, music, and visual artwork. They invited other artists to join them, and that's what brought Michael and his goose to our doorstep.

I showed up at the church one afternoon when Michael was there, and he asked me if I wanted to see what he was working on. I followed him to the balcony, where he showed me an enormous wire framework. It looked like a metal gourd covered with wet paper bags.

"So what's this going to be?" I asked him.

"It's a goose," he nonchalantly responded, as though it was completely normal to build a giant goose on a church balcony.

"It's a what?"

"A goose. I'm going to hang it from the rafters and have it hover over the people."

"Oh."

I mean, what else can a guy say?

Seeing my dismay, he then launched into an explanation. "For Celtic Christians, the goose is the image of the Holy Spirit. They had a phrase, 'The Holy Spirit is like an untamed, wild goose.'"

As soon as he said it, I got it. What a fantastic image: The Holy Spirit, untamed and wild.

On Pentecost Sunday, our community met the goose in its completed glory. It has become such a beautiful image of the life we are trying to live together that I hope it will hover over us for as long as it holds together.

In the version of Christianity I learned, the Holy Spirit is not a goose but rather a gentle, cooing, pristine white dove. And there's certainly something lovely and comforting about that image. Yet for so many of us, life with God isn't the least bit pristine. It is far more like some squawking, unmanageable thing you can't quite get your hands on.

Thinking about the Holy Spirit as a wild goose changes the way we tell the story. Still, for a whole culture of people, a whole collection of Christians, the goose is as normal a symbol for the Holy Spirit as you can get. The early Celts lived with this image for centuries, and it isn't the least bit strange to them. In fact, they might find our dove to be an odd and far-too-domesticated picture of God.

The idea of the wild, untamed Spirit of God hit me with a force no dove could muster. I love that goose because it suggests a different way of thinking about the Christian faith. In that wild goose borrowed from an ancient culture, I see the expansive, expressive, explosive hope that can be found when we are willing to take God out of the cultural cages we've built and let God run free and wild. It isn't just a great piece of art; it is a great piece of theology.

Naturally, there are struggles when we use new ways to talk about Christian faith. But we run into greater problems when we forget that context exists and wrongly assume that the story we have is the pure, unretouched version. Whether we know it or not, the dogmas and doctrines of God, of humanity, of Jesus, of sin, of salvation that many of us were taught are so firmly embedded in the cultural context of another time that they have become almost meaningless in ours.

Whether we know it or not, the dogmas and doctrines that many of us were taught are so firmly embedded in the cultural context of another time that they have become almost meaningless in ours.

Once I caught on that John wrote his gospel as an active evangelist, I began to see that the reason I had such a hard time getting that train car version of faith to hook up with my experience of God was because it was only one of many versions of the story of Jesus. This realization set me on this pursuit of a new theology, one that reflects what I see as the call of all Christians: to seek, live, and tell the story of God's work in the world, to embrace a faith that is alive and vibrant, untamed and uncaged, right here, right now.

5

WHEN DIFFERENT WAS GOOD

From the start, Christianity has been a faith embedded in the lives of its followers. The Christian faith has always been multicultural, meaning it could be lived in a variety of cultures and languages. Christianity has never required everyone to speak a unified language or follow specific cultural customs. Rather the belief has been that the Holy Spirit dwells in and among people and is teaching and guiding communities and individuals in faith. There is a long and rich history of the Christian faith spreading and morphing and taking its cues from the people who live it out. Centuries passed before Christian leaders mandated a unified culture and belief system.

The New Testament tells us that one of the primary issues for early Christians was figuring out how—and if—non-Jewish people could live the promise of God that came through Jesus. Jesus was a Jew, as were most of his original followers. Jesus preached that he was the Messiah who was the fulfillment of the promise made by God to Abraham. This was a Jewish story.

The story held together just fine until Gentiles began converting to Christianity as quickly as Jews. In the first century, Jews thought of people in two categories, Jews and non-Jews, who were called Gentiles (I will often refer to them as Greeks). Since Jesus was a Jew, his Jewish followers assumed that the Gentiles would need to become Jews in order to be Christians. It made perfect sense. They figured that their version of the story was the only one that held up. But over time that understanding changed. The New Testament writers make it clear that it was not only acceptable for Gentiles to follow Jesus as Gentiles but that the inclusion of the Gentiles was the ultimate fulfillment of the promise of God to Abraham—that he would be a blessing to the entire world as "the father of many nations." Christianity was the faith of the many.

This issue was not easily settled. In fact, it was the impetus for the first church "council," held by the early church to answer the question, "Do the Gentiles need to become Jews in order to follow Jesus?" (You can read the story in Acts 15.) This was not some academic pursuit; it was a deeply personal and passionate crisis for many in the faith. The predominant Jewish story was that they were God's chosen people and that anyone who wanted in on the story had to become a Jew. So for many Jews, the idea that Gentiles could enter into the story of God's people without becoming Jews was not just disturbing but downright blasphemous.

The participants at the council determined that indeed Gentiles did not need to convert to Judaism in order to become Christians. It is nearly impossible to convey the implications of this decision—it was an incredibly risky thing to do. The answer would come to have a tremendous impact on the assumptions and practices of the Judaism-based church, including where, when, and how people worshiped. And it took years before the theology behind the decision took hold in the hearts of the believers themselves.

It was James, who is often said to be the brother of Jesus, who concluded the council by saying, "It is my judgment, therefore, that we should not make it difficult for the Gentiles who are turning to God."[1] With this, the church leaders sent a welcome-to-the-faith letter to the Gentile followers and officially decreed that Christianity was not a single-culture faith:

> The apostles and elders, your brothers,
> To the Gentile believers in Antioch, Syria and Cilicia:
> Greetings.
>
> We have heard that some went out from us without our authorization and disturbed you, troubling your minds by what they said. So we all agreed to choose some men and send them to you with our dear friends Barnabas and Paul—men who have risked their lives for the name of our Lord Jesus Christ. Therefore we are sending Judas and Silas to confirm by word of mouth what we are writing. It seemed good to the Holy Spirit and to us not to burden you with anything beyond the following requirements: You are to abstain from food sacrificed to idols, from blood, from the meat of strangled animals and from sexual immorality. You will do well to avoid these things. Farewell.[2]

While this list of requirements may sound odd and capricious to us, it made sense to the Jews and the Gentiles of the first century. From this point on, increasing numbers of the early Christians were evangelized Gentiles, not Jews. The new challenge for the church, then, was how to help Jewish and Gentile Christians unite as co-laborers with God and be one big happy adoptive family. It was in keeping these mandates that Gentiles could enter the synagogue (the meeting place of Jewish communities outside of Jerusalem). So the Jewish believers were asking the Gentile believers to do whatever they could to make it possible for the two groups to meet together. The first few centuries of the Christian faith were all about this balance between diversity and unity.

But then something changed. Historians and theologians debate the details, reasons, and timelines, but within a few centuries a shift took place. Christianity started moving from a faith committed to multicultural unity to one requiring monocultural uniformity. In other words, Christianity began settling into one particular culture and world-view, and all adherents had to convert to that worldview if they wanted to follow Jesus. Strangely, that mandatory worldview was not the Hebrew worldview of the Jewish people. It was the Greek worldview of the Gentiles. It was as if the entire issue had gone full circle—from the early followers of Jesus suggesting that all Gentiles must become Jewish to follow Jesus to the mandate that all people must become Greek-thinking people to be faithful Christians. And this development has wreaked havoc for centuries.

> **Christianity began settling into one particular culture and worldview, and all adherents had to convert to that worldview if they wanted to follow Jesus.**

My daughter, Michon, once said to me, "You know what my favorite Bible story is? The one where the guy is given the vision of the cross on his shield and the voice says, 'By this cross you will conquer!'"

She might as well have said she had started smoking so she could get in better shape.

"That is not a Bible story, honey," I said with a mix of hurt, shock, and horror. "That is a story about what went wrong with Christianity. That is the story of Constantine domesticating the faith by turning it into one of control and dominance."

Unfazed, Michon replied, "Well, I like it. It is a really cool story."

It turns out she'd heard this story from me. Our church had been using a series of sermons to tell the story of Christianity. We were tracing how the faith of the first Christians turned into the very different version of faith we live today. One night we talked about the conversion of Constantine, which is quite a story. In 311 the Roman Empire was divided and different rulers claimed the title of emperor. So Constantine was at war with his counterpart over the throne. According to Constantine, the night before he was to enter the final battle for the mantle of leader of the Roman Empire, he was met by a vision. Looking toward the sun, the Greek letters chi and rho—the first two letters of the Greek name for Christ—and the phrase, "In this sign, conquer," appeared to him. Constantine had his army paint the sign of the cross on their shields in an effort to fulfill this vision. Constantine was victorious in battle and, with a cross in his hand, ascended to the throne as sole emperor of the Roman Empire. This, then, is how the cross became the symbol of Rome. Now no decent emperor was going to be happy with anything short of uniformity and compliance, and this was certainly the case for Constantine. He had wars to win, nations to conquer, and order to keep. He was not interested in diversity in the official religion or anything else. Once Rome claimed Christianity as the state religion, the Hebrew version of the faith was quickly painted over by the Greco-Roman version in order to help it fit with this new cultural setting.

History has proved the idea of a state religion to be a rather troubling development in the Christian story—the institutionalization and coercion that come with empire are not really compatible with the gospel message. But my point is that Michon—like many others before her—was captivated by a story that had the trappings of a vibrant and noble faith. Too often the church has been captivated by moments in our history that should be thought of not as road maps but as warnings.

The Greco-Roman version of Christianity, then, was always a cultural adaptation. It was never meant to replace the Hebrew version. Rather it was intended to help that story make sense to a different set of people—like the Masai creed with the hyenas. But the Jews were the minority in the Roman Empire, so it was their story, not the Greco-Roman story, that was adapted and remade to make sense in this new setting.

> Too often the church has been captivated by moments in our history that should be thought of not as road maps but as warnings.

The Hebrew faith was actually quite prepared make this adaptation. Long before Constantine came along, the Jews were fighting a losing battle to keep their faith free from Greek influence. In the time between the Old and New Testaments, the Old Testament was translated into Greek so that the Jews who were learning Greek would have the Scriptures in their new language. Many Jews living in Jerusalem, which was under Roman occupation, worked for Greeks, lived with Greeks, and even took on Greek names; this explains why many of the characters in the New Testament have both Hebrew and Greek names (Simon is Peter, Saul is Paul). The Greek influence in the Christian world was becoming so strong that the majority of the New Testament was written in Greek, rather than in the ancient languages of the Jews.

In the first century, as Christianity spread from Jerusalem to the rest of the Mediterranean, the followers of Jesus used Greek understandings—ideas, symbols, reference points—to tell the story of the Hebrew faith. They translated the faith into cultural terms that resonated with the Greek experience. This process is called Hellenization (Hellas is the name for Greece in Greek). It means the cultural change in which something non-Greek becomes Greek. This Hellenization had been taking place since the third century, but the Jews had successfully resisted fully taking on the Greek culture as their own. Their faith remained deeply Hebrew, but it was now articulated in the Greek language.

By the time Christianity became the official Roman religion under Constantine, it was so deeply a Greek expression that not only had the Jewish heritage faded, but many Christians were fearful of the Jews, and deep conflict between Jews and Christians was common. This marked quite a change. The influence of telling a dynamic Jewish story in and through multiple cultures was replaced with a Greek monocultural expression of Christianity. It is from within this fully Greek worldview that much of our "official" modern Christianity arose.

I don't for a minute believe that the people who promoted this Greek version of the Christian story were ignorant or malicious or heretical. I think they acted with the best of intentions. But I also know that throughout history, people have missed the point or turned tangents into the main issue—it happens all the time. And when it happens, the trajectory of a story changes.

The church of the early centuries didn't just grab everything in the Greek worldview and Christianize it. These Christians did important theological work with prayer and devotion to make sense of the story of God; they made a real effort to ensure that the culture didn't swallow up the story. Still, the further the church got from the Jewish story of Jesus, the less Hebrew influence there was and the greater the dominance of Greek thought became. The Greeks made Christianity their own—which had been the hope of many of the New Testament Christians from the beginning—but much of the Hebrew story was lost along the way.

As a result, the Greek perspective has come to inform Christian thought about everything from God and Jesus to sin and salvation, for the last seventeen hundred years. In other words, the theology that guides the present-day church is in many ways a version of faith customized for the fifth-century Greco-Romans. And when that view was set in stone as the inarguable, unchanging, only way to explain faith, it cre-

The theology that guides the present-day church is in many ways a version of faith customized for the fifth-century Greco-Romans.

ated all kinds of trouble for those of us living today. Whether we like if or not, whether we are aware of it or not, when the telling of the gospel changes, the meaning of the gospel changes with it. And that's how we have ended up with a changed faith.

Language can change everything. The Greeks had a radically different view of the world from the Hebrews. The Hebrew faith was built around the story of the Old Testament and the nation of Israel, but the Greco-Roman view was based on the ideas of their philosophers. And this change in basic assumptions made all the difference in the world.

See if any of this sounds familiar. The Greek philosophers like Aristotle, Plato, and Socrates believed that God was an abstract force, not a personal father figure. This notion was built on the assumption that there were two forces in the world—flesh and spirit. Spirit was perfect and good. Flesh was limited and needy. The spirit and the flesh were distinct and separate. This all transferred to Greek thinking about God, suggesting that God must be wholly Spirit. Plato concluded that God was perfect, unchanging, and in need of nothing. God existed apart from humanity in a state of divine purity. God's perfection had to be timeless, and therefore God must exist outside of time. God, then, was the best we could imagine, the Ultimate.

Aristotle took Plato's ideas and applied them to the issue of change; it was from his thinking that God became known as the Unmoved Mover. Aristotle argued that there must be some initiating force in the universe that is not in itself affected by other forces. That meant that God was totally insulated from outside knowledge, for God needed nothing. God was characterized by timelessness, immutability, and rationality. Contrast this with the Hebrew story of a God who creates in God's own image, a God who is present and active in the world. It's pretty clear that one view was going to slide into the background.

Philosophers like Philo (20 B.C.–A.D. 50), a Jewish thinker who lived about the same time as Jesus, tried to tell the Jewish story using the Greek language. This effort led him into some linguistic troubles. For example, he explained the story of the Old Testament in Greek terms. But the Greek language didn't have a way of explaining God as the intimate creator—that kind of language simply wasn't used for God. So Philo proposed the image of God as the ultimate gardener or architect—a bit removed, yet still the master over the earth. Other Jewish religious leaders were suspicious of Philo's writings because they seemed far more Greek than Hebrew. Still, Philo was widely accepted by early Greek converts to Christianity, and his views are alive in commentaries and theological scholarship today.

By the time Justin Martyr came along (A.D. 100–165), the Greek perspective was accepted not as a tangent or a missional response but as the primary perspective for understanding the Christian story. Justin concluded that the Christian God was not a new idea at all but a more comprehensive understanding of the Hellenized concept of God. He wrote, "For while we say that all things have been produced and arranged into a world by God, we shall seem to utter the doctrine of Plato . . . not because the teachings of Plato are different from those of Christ, but because they are not in all respects similar, as neither are those of the others, Stoics, and poets, and historians."[3] He goes on to title sections of his explanation of Christianity "Plato's Obligation to Moses" and "Plato's Doctrine of the Cross."

The clash between the Hebrew and Greek perspectives on God and faith created a major problem for fourth- and fifth-century Christians—it was the impetus for the statements of faith, councils, and creeds meant to codify the faith in the first millennium. Christian thinkers had to respond to problems created by the accepted Greco-Roman worldview that was colliding with the Hebrew story of Jesus, which was still the prevailing understanding found in the Bible.

One of the famous Christian theologians of the fifth century was a man named Augustine, perhaps the most influential Christian theologian of all time. Augustine's mother was a Christian, and his father was a pagan. Before his Christian conversion, he was a follower of a belief called Manichaeism, a Platonic religion that required an intense level of commitment to the notion of separating the body and spirit. He was himself a picture of the conflicted interplay of Christianity, paganism, and cultural religion.

Augustine and many who followed him needed to create complex theologies to smooth out the questions raised by all of these competing worldviews. Their theological explanations are brilliant for their situation, but they are just that—situational explanations. They are not in and of themselves the story of God. This is why it's important for us to recognize the cultural encoding that takes place every time a theology is created. Every theology is grounded in a culture and a set of culturally based assumptions and concerns. To hold to these theologies in the fifth century was to be faithful, for they were created as explanations for the understanding of the world at that time. But to hold to those same conclusions today, when the worldview that demanded them has expired, is simply foolish.

We've seen this throughout history. Martin Luther adapted Augustine's theology for sixteenth-century Germany.

John Calvin adapted Augustine's theology for sixteenth-century Switzerland. John Knox adapted it for sixteenth-century Scotland. All three men were taking what they knew of theology—which was a great deal—and re-creating the church in ways that were faithful for their time and place. They were so successful that much of what we know of Augustine's thinking is seen through the lens of these contextual theologians.

Whether we know anything of the particular players in this drama—Augustine, Aristotle, Calvin, or anyone else—we have all been affected by this acceptance of the Greco-Roman concepts of God from the early church and often find it difficult to distinguish them as being anything but "Christian." In many ways this problem takes us back to the issues the first Christians dealt with: Is it necessary to convert to a particular worldview in order to hold the Christian faith? Or in this case, does a person have to be a fifth-century Augustinian in order to be a follower of Jesus? The answer, of course, is no. To paraphrase James from that first council, it is my judgment, therefore, that we should not make it difficult for the non-Greeks who are turning to God.

As I learned this part of my faith's history, it became clear to me where the "unchanging knowledge, absolute assurance" version of faith on my Burger King placemat came from. It was a remnant from the interpretations of the Bible as seen through the lens of Greek philosophy. I'm not suggesting that I was somehow sold a bill of goods when I was discipled in the Christian faith. I'm not even suggesting that we have to strip the Greek worldview from our understanding of Christianity (frankly, this is simply impossible). But I believe that it is the tradition of our faith to constantly renew, rethink, and reformulate our ideas about what it means to follow God. I believe that we can reject the particular Greco-Roman, Platonic, Aristotelian, and Augustinian dogmas about God, humanity, Jesus, sin, and salvation without rejecting the faith. Indeed, we must do so.

Just as the Greco-Roman version of Christianity was not the end point for me, what I'm proposing in this book is not meant to be the final word either. Although our knowledge, perspective, and understandings of the world are more developed than those of our predecessors, I like to think that we are just ten short steps ahead of them on a thousand-mile journey. This vantage point is important and meaningful, but we are by no means infallible. We may know more, and what we know matters, but what we don't know is far greater than what we do know. We may be a bit ahead, but we are not even close to finished. We must put the gospel into forms that serve us well today, but they, too, will one day expire. The generations who come after us will face the task of advancing this journey the next ten steps, taking what we have offered as a trail guide, not a stopping point. They will be called—just as we are, just as Christians have always been—to recognize their context and reimagine their faith.

So as you read, I hope my suggestions stir up new and possibility-filled questions in you. I hope they encourage you, inspire you, and mess with you just enough remind you of the good news that we are part of a faith that is worth believing.

6

IT'S IN THE WAY THAT YOU USE IT

When I was growing up, we had a Bible in the back room of our apartment, near my room. I was probably about ten years old when I found it and opened it up. Somehow I knew it was a religious book, even though I had never been taught anything from it. But it had all the trappings of something special.

It had a simple black cover with nothing but "Holy Bible" written on it. There were no pictures, no author's name. It creaked as I opened it, a dusty smell drifting up from the pages. Everything about it was weird. The size was odd; the paper was strangely thin; the type was tiny. The words were laid out in columns with weird numbers scattered around the page. The ink was mostly black, but halfway through some of it was red. It felt like I'd discovered a dying old relative living in our house. And it gave me the creeps.

It was nearly seven years before I opened a Bible again.

That moment came the day after my experience at the Passion Play. I don't remember if the people backstage suggested we buy Bibles or if I just felt compelled to get one, but I knew I needed to get my hands on that book again. And I knew just where to go.

Being a kid with unusually large feet made buying shoes a real dilemma. The only place to find my size 15 shoes was at the Big and Tall shop at the Foursome Mall. I'd often noticed the churchy store in the mall but never set an oversized foot in the place. Now I couldn't wait to get there. The last time I'd thought about the Bible, it had been like an eccentric old aunt turning brittle in the back room. But this time I felt like I was on my way to pick up my awesome new girlfriend. The twenty-minute drive was twenty minutes too long.

The first few moments in that store were like nothing I'd felt before or since. It was like walking into a secret world filled with images and stories I'd never known existed. I had no idea there was all this stuff about God. There were books, posters, figurines, music albums. And Bibles, so many Bibles. Naturally, I had no idea which one to pick, but I remember thinking, *I need to find one with that crazy column down the middle and the special colored words.* I thought the black cover was ugly, so I settled for a burgundy New American Standard Bible. I went home and started reading.

The salesperson at the bookstore had suggested I start with the New Testament, so I did. I wasn't much of a reader (I didn't read a book from beginning to end until I was in college), but over the next few months, I made my way through the story of Jesus, the story of Paul, the story of the early church. I read my Bible so often and with **These people had what I wanted—life with God. These were the stories of my people.** such ferocity that I'm sure my parents were concerned about me, even though they never said anything about it. I couldn't get enough. I loved these people, these letters, these words. For the most part, I understood what I was reading. But even the places that were puzzling thrilled me. I was reading the narrative of the life I wanted to be living. These people had what I wanted—life with God. These were the stories of my people.

Maybe it's because my Bible experience started out with such intimacy that I love the Bible so deeply. And maybe it was not growing up with the Bible that makes me act like a

Depression-era grandmother at a café shoving packets of sugar in her purse, but I hoard Bibles. I own new ones with fancy covers and niche versions like my hip-hop Bible. I have well-worn Bibles whose margins are filled with my notes and questions. I even have an old family Bible that belonged to my surrogate grandmother, Eleanor, who lived down the hall from our apartment when I was a kid. With its engraved leather cover, metal hinges, and rickety lock, it seems more like an antique than a Bible. These aren't just books to me. They are treasures. They are the stories I love and cling to. They are filled with words of comfort, of hope, of joy. They are powerful and beautiful and life-changing.

So much of what I've come to believe about God and humanity and Jesus and the way we are to live comes from the Bible. For me, it is a living thing. It is a member of my community and a vital source of wisdom and truth. But it's rarely used that way. Which is why I often cringe when I hear someone getting ready to use the Bible.

In my years of being a Christian, I have witnessed the most brutal fights over the Bible. I know families where some members no longer speak to one another because of disagreements over the Bible. I have heard stories of people losing their jobs because they disagree with someone about a biblical principle. Entire denominations have split over disagreements about the "proper" interpretation of the Bible. I have witnessed people saying and doing heinous things with the justification that the Bible made them do it.

As we dig into the theology of the past and the theology I'm proposing for today, I think it's only fair to be upfront about how I read the Bible, how I understand the Bible, and how I use the Bible. If we are going to step into the new expressions and understandings of faith I'm talking about here, it's essential to develop a fuller sense of what I believe the Bible is and what it isn't.

To start with, it is not a weapon. My years at a Christian college were like an anthropology class on evangelicalism—I had a master's level education on the norms of Christian culture. Some of my friends who'd grown up in the church would reminisce about weekly "sword drills" at Sunday school. A few of them even went to national sword drill competitions. Apparently these drills worked like this: The leader would quote a Bible verse without mentioning the reference. The "combatants" would quickly search their Bibles to find the verse. The first person to find it thrust the Bible in the air like a sword raised in victory.

My friends explained that the imagery came from the metaphor Paul used in his letter to the church at Ephesus, the one that reads:

> Therefore put on the full armor of God, so that when the day of evil comes, you may be able to stand your ground, and after you have done everything, to stand. Stand firm then, with the belt of truth buckled around your waist, with the breastplate of righteousness in place, and with your feet fitted with the readiness that comes from the gospel of peace. In addition to all this, take up the shield of faith, with which you can extinguish all the flaming arrows of the evil one. Take the helmet of salvation and the sword of the Spirit, which is the word of God.[1]

So the sword drills took their name from the idea that the Bible is the sword of the Spirit. By then I was well aware of the passage, but I'd never known people who used the language so literally, actually learning the Bible so that it could become a kind of weapon. Then again, back in high school, one of my youth leaders had made the point that the helmet, shield, belt, and breastplate were defensive tools and the Bible was the only offensive tool. (That certainly has proved to be true in my experience. I have never seen someone attacked with the shoes of peace.)

It seemed odd to me then to think about my beloved Bible being used for war. It still is. The thing is, Paul wasn't talking about a war between people. He wrote, "For our struggle is not against flesh and blood, but against the rulers, against the authorities, against the powers of this dark world and against the spiritual forces of evil in the heavenly realms."[2] Yet many of the Christians I know truly believe that we are at war with the human enemies

> It seemed odd to me then to think about my beloved Bible being used for war. It still is.

of our faith. They use the Bible to stab and shred and rip into what they believe to be faulty theology. They wield that weapon in a way that brings pain, suffering, and humiliation.

Yes, the Bible is meant to admonish, to teach, to enlighten. There are certainly times when the Bible calls us to live in a way that is quite different from the way we want to live, and that dissonance provokes pain and struggle. But that struggle comes through the conviction brought on by God's Spirit stirring. It's a very different thing when the Bible is used as a tactical force to beat others into ideological submission. When the Bible is used for such purposes, it is no longer the sword of the Spirit but the sword of spite.

We also need to know what kind of book the Bible is and is not. It is not a reference book. Far too many people—and by that I mean nearly all of us—have a tendency to use the Bible as an encyclopedia. We assume that the Bible is full of truth, so we can just jump to a verse and find something worthwhile. As with any encyclopedia, we don't need to read the preceding submission to get our information. In fact, doing so can actually change the entire meaning of what we've read; if I'm looking for information on **Each time we open the Bible, we are stepping into the work of writers and storytellers, poets and prophets.** the word *façade* and start reading the entry on the *Fabulous Furry Freak Brothers* on the same page, I'm in trouble. When using an encyclopedia, we have to stay on topic.

This is very different from the way we read a novel. We know that if we open up a novel somewhere in the middle and just start reading, we'll not only be lost in the midst of a plot we don't understand, but we might begin to make assumptions about the story that are completely wrong.

It's not hard to see where I'm going with this. The Bible isn't a reference book with stand-alone entries. It's not a collection of short stories that are unrelated to one another. The Bible is a full narrative in which each section is part of a greater story. Each time we open the Bible, we are stepping into the work of writers and storytellers, poets and prophets.

Yet so often we use bits and pieces of the Bible to construct narratives, stories, and systems that suit our purposes. To open the Bible and pluck out verses is like drawing up a house plan without ever looking at the building site. That's very different from living on the land, studying its contours, and building a home that is inspired by and grows out of the site itself. Our call is to look at the entire narrative of the Bible and allow it shape us, not to go in with a preconceived notion of what we think we'll find there.

This extraction method doesn't happen by accident either. I was trained to go into the Bible and get the truth from it. The idea was that inside of all that narrative, behind all the context and culture, was a nugget of truth. My goal as a reader was to find that timeless piece of wisdom, that universally applicable principle, and drop it into the situation at hand. Sometimes this surgical procedure required taking a word from a sentence, other times taking a sentence from a paragraph. If I had a really complicated point to make, I might have to remove sentences from a variety of paragraphs— maybe even paragraphs written by different authors, thousands of years apart—and graft them together. The context wasn't important. In fact, it kind of got in the way.

If I really wanted to dig into the truth hidden in these words and sentences, I could decode the secret languages— Hebrew, Greek, Aramaic—that held the real key to the mysteries of the Bible. No ordinary person could find these secret truths, but I was trained to find them and get them out.

It was like playing the game Operation. When I was a kid, I liked being the "doctor," reaching into the slot on the leg with a steady hand and pulling out the femur bone without touching the sides. I liked the precision of finding something, extracting it, and leaving no trace. That's a great technique for a board game. It's not so great for reading the Bible, a book written and meant to be read by communities of faith.

Those communities matter—both the ancient communities in which the Bible took shape and our present-day communities in which we work to shape our lives around the message of the Bible. It's just plain wrongheaded to try to remove the words of the Bible from their context. The context and culture of the community have everything to do with what's written in the Bible and how we read it and live it.

I recently had an exchange with a pastor friend of mine who argued that using references without regard to their entire context is exactly what Jesus and the apostles did. He cited instances where Jesus refers to a teaching of Moses without reciting the entire book of Exodus and places where Jesus quotes Isaiah without using the whole prophetic speech. He reminded me that the apostles connected events in their lives to ancient prophecies and didn't concern themselves with filling in the whole history of the prophet. So, my friend argued, this practice is not only justified but exemplified in the Bible.

He made a good point. Jesus and the apostles often quoted from the Old Testament. And frankly, the connections they make to past writings are quite a stretch sometimes. Yet their references to the Old Testament were never meant as a way of skipping over important parts of the story or condensing the story for their listeners. Jesus and the apostles were connecting their stories with those that had come before. They were alluding to what had been said and done in an effort to trace the arc of the story they were living. It was the context that made these words meaningful.

It's also worth noting that the people listening to Jesus and the apostles didn't need to be told the context of the references to Moses or Isaiah; they already knew it. They knew the rest of the Moses story. They knew the rest of Isaiah's prophecy. When Jesus quotes Moses as saying that one should honor one's father and mother, he doesn't explain the entire Law of Moses; the people he is talking to know it by heart. The Bible wasn't an ancient book to them; it was the living history of their people. It was impossible for them to listen to Jesus, to listen to the apostles, without knowing the full context of the words being spoken.

But when a pastor in Minneapolis pulls a passage from Exodus 20, finds the "core" meaning of it, and then builds additional thinking around it from some passages in Isaiah and her own Sunday school upbringing, she is doing something new. I know there are times when this is what's needed to make a point or start a conversation. And I have done it myself on occasion (I've even done it in this book—there are times when brevity requires this approach). But when we pull pieces of the Bible out of their context, when we add to them or fit them together in new ways, we need to be honest about what we're doing and acknowledge that we are changing the meaning of those pieces.

This practice of selective quoting can be helpful, but most of the time, it creates confusion and misunderstanding. It messes up our sense of the overall story. This is true not only with the Bible but with all communication. There are times when my children tell me something my wife, Shelley, has said. They typically give me a synopsis rather than a word-for-word account, removing many of the details of the conversation to communicate more clearly. But there are times when their condensed version of the report is actually a changed version, which leads to frantic phone calls between Shelley and me trying to figure out why the plans I thought we had are so drastically different from the plans playing out. Knowing how frustrating it is to be misunderstood, I sometimes wonder if God ever wants to yell, "Hey, that's not what I was trying to say!" or if the apostle Paul would find himself in great disagreement with sermons preached from his words. Actually, I don't wonder. I am quite sure that's the case.

The encyclopedic approach leads to something else the Bible is not. It is not a list of quotes to be memorized. In the early days of my faith, a dear friend of mine, who was big into memorizing passages from the Bible, gave me a set of cards with Bible verses on them and encouraged me to memorize all of the verses. It was quite a set of cards—there must have been hundreds of 'em. My friend shared his memorization system with me: say the reference; quote the verse; say the reference again.

Every time I saw this friend, he'd ask, "So what verse are you working on?" No kidding, every time. Mostly my answer would be, "The same one as last time we met," by which I meant none. Or I would say, "John 3:16, but I can't remember how it goes," just to get under his skin. He would say, "Dougie, you know how important this is." And he meant it. For him, this was a crucial practice that allowed him to structure his faith, to feel like he was always working and growing as a Christian.

One day I got up the nerve to admit that I didn't like the verse-memorizing method, that I preferred the narrative story approach. I was new to all this faith stuff but already knew it was bigger than a bunch of verses. He didn't really understand what I was talking about and didn't agree when I explained it to him. The conversation turned rather heated, and although we didn't exactly end our friendship, it was never the same after that.

There is little doubt that my friend's approach is much more the norm than mine. People use all kinds of techniques to learn Scripture, from Sunday school drills to "verse of the day" calendars to taping verses to the bathroom mirror. The Christian publishing industry has produced comprehensive systems to help people memorize the Bible—Bibles with learning plans, CDs for kids with verses set to music, handy cards to carry in a briefcase, and on and on.

For people who find this practice an important part of their faith, I suppose these products are helpful. But there's an unspoken message in all that memorization: In picking hundreds of verses as the ones we should learn, we are saying something about the ones we leave out. By one count, there are 31,103 verses in the Bible. So when I considered memorizing 300 of them, I was aiming at getting one percent of them in my heart. Sure, one percent is better than zero percent, but we need to ask, "Why those verses? What I am I missing? Is this approach giving me a skewed understanding of the Bible?"

Again, I am not saying it's bad to quote the Bible or memorize it. I'm just saying that in choosing some verses and not others, we are inserting ourselves into the message of the Bible. We are creating a certain interpretation of what the

Bible says. We can't select pieces of the Bible and then claim we are learning—or understanding—the whole thing.

I struggle with the Bible as a weapon, the Bible as an encyclopedia, the Bible as a collection of verses because these approaches strip the Bible of its meaning and intent. The Bible is a dynamic story of life and faith. But these simplistic methods of study take what was meant to be a life-giving force for believers and threaten to turn it into a dead, meaningless muddle of words. What makes this even more troubling for me is that the people who use the Bible in these ways tend to be the very people who argue for a rigid, authoritarian understanding of the Bible.

Christians have long defended the Bible against those who claim it is useless because it is filled with myths and fiction. But in recent years that battle has moved from being one between Christians and non-Christians to a battle within Christianity itself. I've come to believe that this battle has little to do with the Bible and more to do with certain beliefs many Christians want to keep intact. The Bible becomes justification for their position. This is particularly true on the topics such as homosexuality and the role of women.

I know that saying this is going to raise some hackles, but I think there are people who argue for an "inerrant" authoritative understanding of the Bible to support their prejudiced feelings about homosexuals. I know they would deny it, and they have done so to me many times. They would argue that it works the other way—the Bible teaches certain ideas about homosexuality, so that's what they believe.

Maybe so. But it just seems so odd that their beliefs on other biblical topics are not so pronounced. I have rarely had a conversation about the ills of gossip based on the authority of the Bible. I've had even fewer conversations in which people suggest the church should be actively working to eliminate obesity as a form of gluttony because the Bible clearly condemns it. Nor are people concerned about slander simply because Paul warns against it. And despite the Bible's deep and continual concern for the poor, I rarely have conversations in which people use the authority of the Bible to make a case for economic justice.

But on the issue of homosexuality, something strange happens. If the subject at hand is the authority of the Bible, someone invariably asks what I think about homosexuality. If the subject is homosexuality, someone invariably asks what I think about the authority of the Bible. There must be some connection. It makes me wonder if people would argue about the authority of the Bible if it had nothing to say about homosexuality.

Regardless, this authority question is worth looking at, if only because it is such a hot button in Christian circles. So here's how I see it: The Bible gains its authority from God and the communities who grant it authority. Like many people, I believe in the Bible because I believe in God. But I know plenty of people who think it ought to happen the other way around, that a person needs to believe the Bible *in order to believe* in God. So they'll give a Bible to a non-Christian in the hope that by reading about God, that person will be enlightened. Certainly that can happen, but it seems kind of backward to me. I mean, what possible reason would someone have for believing this story if they didn't already believe in God?

I just don't think the Bible is always the best starting point for faith. Abraham didn't believe the Bible when God claimed him to be a righteous man because it hadn't been written yet. Moses didn't read the lived history of his people as devotional material. David didn't meditate on the words of Isaiah. The disciples didn't read the letters of Paul in between conversations with Jesus. The Bible, both the Old and New Testaments, came along in the midst of the story. It is the result of the story of faith, not the cause.

This is usually the point in a conversation where someone starts accusing me of a low view of the Bible, of stripping it of its authority. But I believe this understanding of the Bible restores its authority by allowing it to be alive and free of the constraints we throw on it.

The inerrancy debate is based on the belief that the Bible is the word of God, that the Bible is true because God made it and gave it to us as a guide to truth. But that's not what the Bible says. In a letter from the apostle Paul to a young ministry worker named Timothy, Paul wrote, "All Scripture is God-breathed and is useful for teaching, rebuking, correcting and training in righteousness, so that all God's people may be thoroughly equipped for every good work."[3] Many Christians have taken this phrase to mean that the Bible is made up of God's words. That's not how Paul or Timothy would have understood it. The word *breath* would have brought to mind God as creator and life-giver. In that word they would have heard hints of God speaking, breathing the world into existence in the Genesis story. They would imagine God breathing life into Adam. They would picture Jesus breathing the Holy Spirit on the disciples. For them the image of God's breath symbolized a living and activating force.

Paul and Timothy didn't hold to a faith constrained by a book but to a faith in the living God speaking to them, leading them. Since context matters, it's worth looking at the context of this phrase. Paul wrote:

> You, however, know all about my teaching, my way of life, my purpose, faith, patience, love, endurance, persecutions, sufferings—what kinds of things happened to me in Antioch, Iconium and Lystra, the persecutions I endured. Yet the Lord rescued me from all of them. In fact, everyone who wants to live a godly life in Christ Jesus will be persecuted, while evildoers and impostors will go from bad to worse, deceiving and being deceived. But as for you, continue in what you have learned and have become convinced of, because you know those from whom you learned it, and how from infancy you have known the Holy Scriptures, which are able to make you wise for salvation through faith in Christ Jesus. All Scripture is God-breathed and is useful for teaching, rebuking, correcting and training in righteousness, so that all God's people may be thoroughly equipped for every good work.[4]

For Paul and Timothy, Scripture found its power in the community of faith, in the activity of God as seen through people, in the continuing story of God's partnership with humanity. Paul points to events in his life—his teaching, his persecution, his love. He wants Timothy to understand that this is the life of a believer. And it's in this life that Timothy will truly partner with God.

Paul explains that the Bible, the God-breathed Scriptures, are meant to be lived. The Bible is a functional book that equips people to join with God in God's work so they can act righteously. For Paul, the Holy Scriptures were alive;

God was creating and re-creating through them. The Bible wasn't a removed "truth text." It was a fully integrated piece of the Christian life, one that held authority because it was a living, breathing symbol of God's continual activity.

That perspective has shaped the way I read my Bibles. When my children were young, I couldn't hear the story of Abraham being called to sacrifice Isaac. I don't mean I couldn't listen to it; I mean I couldn't hear it. My terrible fear that something would happen to my son or daughter, my fear that there might be a time when I couldn't protect them, made it impossible for me to hear any-thing of value from that story. On the other hand, when my dad died, I was uniquely tuned into Jesus' saying to the grieving sister

The living Bible invites us to step into the stories, not as observers, but as participants in the faith that is alive and well and still being created.

of a dead man, "I am the resurrection and the life." This is how it works. We are characters in the stories we choose and the stories we hear. The living Bible invites us to step into the stories, not as observers, but as participants in the faith that is alive and well and still being created.

STRANGE MEDICINE

7

r. Pagitt, I would strongly recommend you have an exam done by a urologist." Well there it was, the thing most men never want to hear from an infertility doctor. Shelley and I had two children, who were two and three years old at the time, so we knew we could get pregnant. But the third time was not a charm. So I took the doctor's advice and visited the urologist (which unfortunately had all the bad vibes I had imagined, including the phrase "OK, you can wipe that off and pull up your pants now"). That appointment confirmed what our infertility doctor had suspected: I had a low-grade urinary tract infection. It wasn't the cause of the infertility, he told us, but it was something I should take care of.

The cause of the infertility was much more significant. Shelley was diagnosed with a severe case of endometriosis—so severe that her gynecologist recommended Shelley have a complete hysterectomy as soon as possible.

Within weeks, Shelley had the surgery, theoretically the only way to eliminate the endometriosis. We were told this course of action had a 99 percent chance of successfully treating the disease. Unbelievably, Shelley was part of that 1 percent, and her endometriosis returned.

After working with all kinds of doctors to figure out what to do next, we were referred to the famed Mayo Clinic. The consultation from Mayo ended with the same advice we'd been given from the beginning: "Refine a hormone regimen, and you can manage this disease." But Shelley wasn't interested in disease management. She was interested in a cure.

In a desperate effort to find a solution, Shelley talked with all sorts of people, including Carol, the wife of one of the pastors at the church where I worked. Carol had experienced great success working with a naturopath, something Shelley and I had never heard of. But with nothing to lose, Shelley went to see Dr. Tatiana Riabokin. It was the start of an entirely new phase in our lives.

Dr. Riabokin gave Shelley holistic, natural, nonhormonal options for treating her disease and offered a host of suggestions for eliminating it altogether. Perhaps more important, she provided a possible explanation for why Shelley's disease came on when it did. Shelley's mom was killed in a car accident shortly after the birth of our second child, and the physical shock put her body into crisis and allowed the disease, which had previously been present to a small degree, to grow rapidly. I believe Dr Riabokin's counsel saved Shelley's life, not only physically, but emotionally and spiritually as well.

Until Shelley's illness came along, I had never been one to question my doctors. I went in when something was wrong with my body, they told me what to do about it, and I got better. It wasn't a formula that needed changing. Until, of course, it did. In our pursuit of answers about Shelley's health, we found ourselves asking new questions, questions the members of the established medical community didn't answer.

It wasn't that they couldn't or wouldn't tell us what was going on. The problem was that the whole mentality of Western medicine is based on a set of assumptions and expectations and ideas that take the conversation about health care in a certain direction. We wanted to have a *different* conversation, one that involved a different set of assumptions and expectations and ideas than the illness management conversation.

Expressing our interest in more integrated, holistic options was like speaking a foreign language. The fact that our conversation diverged from that of our regular doctors wasn't their fault. It wasn't our fault. It wasn't anyone's fault any more than it's my fault that I speak English and my friends in Guatemala speak Spanish. The issue wasn't that the doctors were just being old-fashioned or closed-minded. It's that we began asking questions they simply weren't equipped to answer. But the more we dug into natural health alternatives, the more we felt like we'd arrived at the motherland.

Of course, that's not how it felt at first. After a year or so of Shelley's making regular visits to Dr. Riabokin, I remained skeptical of the alternative approach. Shelley would talk about treatment plans based on an integrated view of the body or about the use of herbs and different foods for healing. It was all just a little too weird to me. To make things worse, Dr. Riabokin advised Shelley to get rid of all the white sugar and homogenized milk in our house. Now, for a guy who can barely fall sleep at night without a bedtime bowl of cereal, this Dr. Riabokin was becoming nothing but trouble.

Shelley was convinced that not only was this approach good for her but it would help me find a healthier life as well. She would go on and on about how this was truly health creation and not illness management. After a number of months of unbearable pressure from Shelley and a few of her fellow converts to natural health, I set up an introductory exam with Dr. Cereal Killer.

From the moment I walked into the building for my appointment, I felt out of my element. The clinic was in a renovated old house in downtown Hopkins, Minnesota—just a few blocks from the Burger King of placemat fame. The house had a squeaky floor and a distinct smell of patchouli. The entire thing was just absurd—who sees a doctor in an old house? I was only there because Dr. C.K. had done so much good for Shelley and it was important to my wife that I give it a chance.

I didn't have the religious concerns about the natural health field that some people in my Christian circle had; they were gravely concerned about the dangers of this "New Age" approach. The message was that people being helped by this kind of treatment were somehow just not seeing things clearly, that anyone who suggested that the body is designed to heal itself was simply wrong or, worse, unbiblical. There were those who suggested that if there was anything to this holistic approach, it might be spiritual, but it certainly wasn't from God.

But I wasn't afraid of my soul being compromised or my mind being opened to evil influences. My problem was that I just didn't buy it. From what I had heard of the whole thing, there was just no way it could work.

When the attendant called my name, I went to the back of the house and entered an exam room. I was surprised to see that the room looked and felt like a real doctor's office; there was an examining table and everything. But when the attendant closed the door behind me, I started to freak out a bit. On the wall was a set of shelves filled with dozens of little glass bottles, each with a white paper label on it. I walked over to see if any of them said "eye of newt," but before I could find out, the door opened and Dr. C.K. came in.

She had a wonderful presence about her—calm, personable, not at all quackish. We started the session by talking about why I was there. I wanted to say, "For starters, I would like my cereal back." But I simply said, "I'm here to appease my wife."

"So do you have anything in particular troubling you?" she asked. It had been more than a year since my infertility appointment, and I hadn't done anything about that urinary tract infection. I had never even mentioned it to Shelley because she had enough to worry about at the time. So I really didn't want to get it on record with Shelley's doctor. "No," I said. "Nothing in particular is troubling me."

Dr. C.K. started her exam by having me lie on my back with my hands at my sides. She was quite particular about the position of my body—where my arms were, if my knees were bent, that kind of thing. She began putting those creepy little bottles in my left hand and asking me to position my other arm in certain ways. She had me lift my left arm above my chest while lying on my back. She turned my wrist a bit and then pulled on my arm, determining the amount of resistance. For the first few minutes I just lay there thinking, *What could she possibly be doing?* Then I noticed that the slightest changes in the position of my right hand seemed to make a difference in her readings of the resistance on my extended arm.

Every now and then Dr. C.K. would offer up a "hmmm" and then turn around, grab three more bottles, and move them quickly in and out of my hand, pulling on my left arm like a retiree at a slot machine. I asked her what was in the bottles. "Elements that might be good for your internal organs," she said as though that explained everything.

Now I was really convinced this was a sham. How could something in my hand, inside a bottle, tell her anything about the organs inside my body? When I asked her about this, she said, "It's based on the resistance from your left arm. The greater the resistance, the better it is for you."

At this point I just about got off the table. This was 1995, and I had never heard anything so improbable in my entire life. I knew I didn't know everything, but I was a reasonably informed guy. I figured that if there was anything to this casino-floor diagnostic tool, I certainly should have heard about it before.

My assumption was that Dr. C.K. was the one who was way off track. Since her approach was, in my mind, just a little sidebar to the broader story of health care, I figured she was the one who was missing the point.

But as I eventually learned, sometimes the people on the edges are the ones making the most sense.

As I eventually learned, sometimes the people on the edges are the ones making the most sense.

The field of holistic health care is based on the idea that the body is an interconnected whole. Pain or sickness in one part of the body is treated as a systemic problem, not an isolated one; instead of saying, "My hand hurts," the holistic-minded person would say, "There's pain in my body that's manifesting itself in my hand." So a holistic doctor does more than check out the hand; she puts little bottles of who-knows-what in it to find out what's going on in the body.

While that theory may sound completely ridiculous— and believe me, I thought it was—in fact, it reflects the reality of nature far more accurately than a perspective that wants to break everything into distinct little packages. Think about creation for a minute. Nothing in the natural world stands in isolation. The quality of the water affects the quality of the earth, which affects the quality of the plants, which affects the quality of the air, which affects the quality of the water. There is connection, interdependence, integration.

The connections in the natural world don't end with what we can see. They reach into the deepest, most elemental structures of matter. Back in the early 1980s, my high school physics teacher taught me that matter was made up of atoms, essentially little hard balls that rest on each other to make stuff. This made perfect sense to me. I threw a baseball at someone, and there was something to catch. If he didn't catch it, all those hard balls might break his nose. I sat on a chair, and something was holding me up. If the hard balls gave way, there was another set ready to catch me when I hit the floor.

I had no trouble believing in these little balls. For years I believed in electrons circling around a hard nucleus. I believed it all until I found out that scientists had stopped believing it and it simply wasn't true.

In the past few decades, science has moved beyond the solid atom to find a far more complex understanding of the material world. Gone are the hard balls. In their place are packets of energy that shift and mingle and move and change. Coming to grips with the idea that at its core solid matter might not be solid at all has been one of the most mind-bending experiences of my life. How can a stable world be made of moving energy?

At the risk of coming across as Bill Nye, the Science Guy, I think it's helpful to run through a brief overview of the nature of, well, nature. In the simplest terms, we now know that at their smallest level, all things are made up of particles of energy. All of these particles have mass, electric charge, and spin, and each particle has an antimatter particle with the same mass and spin but a different electrical charge. When the particle meets the antiparticle, they explode in a flash of energy. But something else happens: particles change their spin, which means they are interacting with particles of the same mass and charge but a different spin. It is the interaction of these particles and the energy released in the interactions that creates stability. (Energy pushes against other energy a bit like two magnets resisting each other.) Rather than thinking of matter being made up of little hard balls resting on one another, the world is made "solid" by the interaction of the energy between active, moving particles. The idea that the material world is made of energy and activity was as weird to me the first time I heard it as it is right now as I write this sentence. The more I've read about fermions, quarks, quantum physics, and nanoscience, the more these ideas have gelled into something that not only makes sense from a scientific perspective but from a theological perspective as well.

What we interact with in a normal day is not all there is; there's more going on than we can see. And what we see and experience is not always the same—there is change in the midst of what appears to be solid. The realization that it is interaction and change that make the world stable has given me new ways to think about the interaction between God and people, people and creation, creation and God. It has released me from thinking of the spiritual world as one thing and the material world as something else. Instead, I have started to get my head around this idea that everything is made of the same stuff, the same energy, interaction, and movement. This understanding has acted as a decoder ring to help me make sense of the pieces of belief that didn't seem to fit into what I was taught.

The realization that it is interaction and change that make the world stable has given me new ways to think about the interaction between God and people, people and creation, creation and God.

Some of those pieces have been floating around inside of me all of my life. In the early days of my faith, I kept hoping Christianity would help them settle into place. When that didn't happen, I assumed that it was because there was something I just wasn't getting, that I was too thick-headed to find the answers I was hoping for. But even after years of education at a Christian college and seminary, these questions, these ideas about who I believed God to be and how I was connected to God were still there. Not only were they still there, but they'd been joined by a whole batch of new questions no one in my religious system seemed willing or able to answer.

That's where I was at when Dr. C.K. came along and sent my head reeling. Once she told me what she was doing with those little bottles, I decided to have a little fun with the exam. I started making subtle changes, like closing one eye while she moved my arm. Then I crossed the toes on my right foot. Dr. C.K paused and then moved my arm again. She kept moving back and forth between bottles, switching them more and more quickly while I was crossing and uncrossing my toes. She finally said, "Hmm, that doesn't make any sense."

"I was crossing my toes," I confessed.

"Well, don't do that," she said. "I think you might have a low-grade urinary tract infection, but I can't tell unless you're still."

How did she know? There was just no way those little bottles could tell her I had an infection. They were as removed from my urinary tract as anything could be. They weren't part of my body or even attached to my body, so how could they offer any information about my body? The more she described the condition and what could be done about it, the more I kept thinking, *How did you do that?*

Dr. Riabokin explained, "Your entire body is connected— your spirit, your emotions, your body, the whole thing. You are a whole being, and there are ways to know what's happening in one part of you by looking at another part." I laid there staring at her, not sure how to take this in. If she hadn't just diagnosed my infection, I would have laughed at her or even argued with her. But I had nothing to say. She smiled and said, "That's just the way things are."

As I drove home, that line kept playing in my head: *That's just the way things are.* Was it? So why did I think my arm was so separate from my spleen? Or assume that my thoughts were just in my head or that my body was one thing and my spirit another? Why had I concluded that I was this collection of distinct parts and not a whole being?

This experience became so disquieting for me that I couldn't stop thinking about it. I started to wonder about the implications of my dualistic mind-set not only on my beliefs about my health but also on my life, my faith, God, the gospel, and what it means to be human. I was a fully trained pastor, for crying out loud! How did I miss this? My introduction to holism seemed like it was about to be one of those major uh-ohs, and I wasn't sure I was ready for that.

8

TOGETHER, AGAIN

That day in Dr. Riaboken's office sent me on a new journey based on new questions that would lead to new answers. Although the integration model I was finding in science and natural health was exciting and inspiring in many ways, it also put me at odds with my faith. The Christianity I'd been taught was built around a dualistic disconnection: we are to be "in the world but not of it." The world is not our home. There are those who have the spirit of God and those who don't. We are one thing, and those other people are, well, other.

Think about the categories we use to talk about faith. There are categories for people—Christians or non-Christians. There are categories for Christians—Catholics or Protestants. There are categories for Protestants—conservative or liberal. The dividing goes on and on—earthly or spiritual, religious or secular, orthodox or heretical. Of course, these categories imply not only distinction but conflict as well: flesh against spirit, God separate from creation, God apart from humanity. God and the spiritual realm stand on one side, and fallen, earthly humans stand on the other.

This language of separation is ingrained in the way many of us think about and talk about Christianity. And it isn't accidental or unintentional. It is often a crucially important starting point to faith. We make an effort to clarify the distinctions between the spiritual and the temporal, the holy and the profane, the human and the divine. This is the kind of separation-based thinking that made sense for those who held to the Greek idea of the distinct, divided nature of flesh and spirit. As with most theology, I believe this dualistic understanding came to us with the best of intentions. But once we have an understanding of the interconnection of all things, that dualism ceases to be useful.

We talked about this very issue in one of my theology classes in seminary. We were tackling the "Love the Lord your God" sections of the gospels, exploring the controversy created by the ways three of the writers quote Jesus. The question on the table was this: How ought we best understand human beings—in two parts, three parts, or even four?

We created a big chart with each passage written out. After each one, we noted the view the writer seemed to hold, or at least what the writer believed Jesus was telling him he should hold.

Matthew quotes Jesus as saying, "Love the Lord your God with all your heart and with all your soul and with all your mind."[1]

Apparently Matthew was a triplist: heart, soul, and mind.

Mark's version goes like this: "Love the Lord your God with all your heart and with all your soul and with all your mind and with all your strength."[2] Mark seems to be a quadralist: heart, soul, mind, strength (the body perhaps?).

And then there's Luke: "Love the Lord your God with all your heart and with all your soul and with all your strength and with all your mind."[3] Same list as Mark, but in a different order. Is that significant?

The mere fact that these entities were written out in list form somehow indicated to us that they had to be distinct from each other. We ran with this assumption with great enthusiasm, never considering whether humans might in fact be whole, integrated beings. There was plenty of discussion of being dualist or a triplist or a quadralist, but being a holist never came up. And the odd thing is that the point of Jesus' call was for people to love God with every part of their life. There is no way to love with only your heart or only your mind. Jesus was casting a vision of a holistic connection with God and with others and our disposition to separation caused us to miss it.

Even with holism sitting at the core of the Jesus message, dualism has been the temptation, and for many the default theology, in Christianity since the first centuries when it was called Gnosticism.

Although Gnostics came in many varieties, there were two primary sects. One was built on the notion that there are two forces at work in the universe, light and darkness. These two fight their battle in the material world, and eventually, light wins. The other approach held that the physical world was created by a lesser god and the spiritual world by the true God. The physical world, therefore, is inferior to the spiritual world. Because the soul is part of the spiritual world, it is superior to the body—at least it will be when it is freed from the confines of the body. The heart, mind, and body are temporary, but the soul is forever. It follows, then, that God is more concerned about the soul than the body, and so we should be as well. These two worlds stand in competition with one another, and it's clear which side we're supposed to be on.

Interestingly, this thinking created plenty of problems for the church. In the fifth century, Augustine, who himself had converted from a group with deeply Gnostic beliefs, attempted to correct the idea that the soul was enslaved by the body. For Augustine, the soul and body created a composite, but the soul ruled over the body as the better of the two. This didn't fully shift the church into an understanding of the human as a whole being—the soul and body were equal but still separate—but Augustine believed it to be a tremendous improvement over the fully dualistic notions of the Gnostics.

The long tentacles of Gnosticism continue to grip the church today. Consider the conversations we have about missions and outreach. Some Christians continue to ask if it is enough to provide for the physical needs of **The long tentacles of Gnosticism continue to grip the church today.** the poor and the oppressed or if it is more important to tend to their spiritual needs. Even those who believe that both are needed are living with these continuing assumptions about the dual nature of human beings.

At our church, we have multiple ways of trying to be useful in the lives of people in need. We help Guatemalan farmers—men and women who have suffered from generations of poverty—find ways to own their homes. We plan events meant to help people in our community move toward health and healing. We participate in a citywide project that provides food for the working poor. We have run tutoring programs and food pantries in the poorest part of Minneapolis. We are committed to bringing an end to human trafficking in our city and around the world. We have done most of these while offering very little of what some Christians might think of as "soul evangelism" to the people we help. We haul cement blocks and talk about decreasing the sugar in their diets and cook chili for them, but not as a cover for talking about the "really important" spiritual issues. All of this leads some people to ask why we put this kind of focus on such "temporal" things rather than focusing on the important issues of eternity and the soul. There is the sense that the work we're doing is nice, but it doesn't really count unless it's a means to a greater end.

I'm not trying to make the case that meeting physical needs is as important as meeting spiritual needs. I'm making the case that there is no difference, that there are not separate categories of need, that when we minister to people, we minister to the whole person. This is the implication of holism, not that we pick one side of the old debate between caring for physical needs and caring for the soul but that we understand and live in the reality that the "difference" between them is not what we may have thought it was.

It's quite easy to accept this idea as a theory. It's much, much harder to break away from the ways in which our Christian language and belief system depend on this understanding. Doing so requires us to step away from assumptions we might not even know we have.

Recently, I was talking about holistic understanding with a friend from our church named Sven. He recounted an event that took place a few years earlier on one of our trips to Guatemala. In the course of our conversation, it became clear that he was skeptical of holistic approaches to healing. He said mockingly, "Holism, yeah, like the time when Erin, the chiropractor, healed Bjorn's sore knee just by holding on to it." (For the record, these are real names. This is, after all, Minnesota.) "Bjorn told us, 'Well I'm not sure if my knee is better, but it does feel warmer.'" Sven took Bjorn's comment to be a statement on the impact of this holistic method.

So I said, "I don't know about Bjorn's knee, but I do know that people who work in holistic health speak about directing energy around the place of the wound."

Sven said, "So they, like, find the soul in the body and direct it to the injury?" His statement was part scoffing and part wondering what I meant.

I said, "Isn't it possible that the body and soul aren't separate at all? It's not like the body is the container that the soul lives in until it is freed."

From the long pause that followed, I was pretty sure I'd hit Sven with something he hadn't really thought about before—and he wasn't buying it. So I finally said, "That notion probably should have gone out of date about the time people realized the earth wasn't flat." He laughed, and we changed the subject.

> **Unfortunately, the notion of the body being a container for the soul hasn't gone out with the other outdated understandings of the natural order.**

Unfortunately, the notion of the body being a container for the soul hasn't gone out with the other outdated understandings of the natural order. It's odd to me that we've let go of so many other expired beliefs once held even by people of deep and thoughtful Christian faith. We no longer think of the earth as a flat disk with a dome of stars sitting over it. We no longer believe the earth is the center of the universe. We no longer believe our galaxy is the only one. Yet separatist dualism has stubbornly survived. And it might just be that people of Christian faith are the ones propping it up.

This separatist understanding is not always innocent. The dark and dirty underbelly of dualism is that it creates in us a kind of hatred for ourselves and for the world. A friend of mine puts it best. He says, "I was told to live in the world the way I tell my kids to act when they have to use a public restroom: get in, get out, and touch as little as possible."

In the same way, separatist thinking breeds the belief that while in the body, human beings are damaged, broken, dirty scum. When I'd been a Christian for about nine months, someone told me about how the great apostle Paul struggled with his flesh and its inherent evil. This guy told me that Jesus himself struggled until he was freed from the confines of his body in the resurrection. The message was obvious: your body is the enemy.

As a seventeen-year-old in the last stages of puberty, I resonated completely with this image of a war between my desire to follow God and the temptations of my adolescent flesh. I had this sense of my soul being chained to my body, unable to be fully engaged with God until that chain was broken. I wanted desperately to feel connected to God, but my new faith made it clear that that wasn't possible as long as I was confined to my body. I would have to wait.

The message of loathing wasn't limited to humanity in some generic sense. It was intended to protect the faithful from the influence of dangerous outsiders. I was encouraged to separate myself from those who weren't "spiritually alive." (This term was yet another reminder of the body-spirit disconnect.

It was one thing to be physically alive, but only some of us got upgraded to spiritually alive.) Those base-level people had no connection to God, so they too were part of the problem. The good news was reduced to "the world is your enemy, the people who don't believe the way you do are the enemy, and even your body, from which there is no escape, is the enemy."

This version of the Christian story seems far removed from the story of the God of the Hebrews, who wept over the people like a heartbroken parent; from the story of Jesus, who befriended "sinners," who touched and healed and loved those considered outcasts, and who interacted with the wind and the rain and the storms at sea; from the story of life and love upending the reign of death and fear.

Which brings me back to those particles of energy. As Christians, we believe we can know God by the nature of the universe and know the nature of the universe by what we know of God. Some of the most beautiful passages in the Bible are found in the Psalms, where David writes about the God of creation. Psalm 36:6 reads, "Your righteousness is like the highest mountains, your justice like the great deep." Psalm 98:8 reads, "Let the rivers clap their hands, let the mountains sing together for joy." Psalm 139:13–14 reads, "For you created my inmost being; you knit me together in my mother's womb. I praise you because I am fearfully and wonderfully made; your works are wonderful, I know that full well." God is connected to the mountains, the oceans, the forests, the tiniest human embryo.

The psalmist certainly isn't promoting pantheism, and neither am I. Rather, I am pointing to this Creator-cosmos congruency. Christians have long used nature and creation as means of connecting with God. Early in my Christian life, I was in a fellowship group that used a booklet to help people understand the Christian faith. The booklet started like this: "Just as there are physical laws that govern the universe, so are there spiritual laws that govern our relationship with God." Without getting into the fact that this statement was based on out-of-date Newtonian "laws" that had already been replaced by more accurate "probabilities and possibilities," it was the idea of cohesion that stuck with me—just as creation, so the Creator.

There is symmetry between the Creator and the created. Creation finds its being in God. Connection is more that a cool idea. It is more than a warm, fuzzy way of talking about Christian community. Connection, interdependence, and integration are woven into the very fabric of creation. I believe that God designed it that way, and I **There is symmetry between the Creator and the created. Creation finds its being in God.** believe that this design tells us something about the way we are to live as part of God's creation.

Christianity isn't a faith that sits in tension with the realities of the world; it is the viewfinder through which our vision of reality finally becomes clear. Once I started thinking about and experiencing Christianity through the lens of holistic connection, I understood it in a completely new way. For example, there's a passage in the Old Testament called the *Shema*. It is in Deuteronomy 6:4 and says, "Hear, O Israel: The LORD our God, the LORD is One." Jews used to begin each day by saying the Shema—and many still do. The passage is a core concept in Judaism and certainly would have been central for Jesus. It forms the basis of the Jewish understanding of God and God's relationship with creation. It is a statement that God is *one*. This was crucial to the Jews and meets with what we know about the reality of the universe. There is unity.

The Bible tells the story of the integration of all things: What was broken is made whole. What was isolated is included. What was out of order is brought into the process. The gospel is about repair, restoration, renewal. It is about completion and cohesion. All the fragments of humanity are brought back together in Jesus.

Contrary to the assumptions of the Greek version of faith many of us have come to know, the good news of Christianity is that we are integrated with God, not separated from God. We tell of being part of creation, not at war with creation. We tell of being connected to one another, not establishing distance from one another. The

The good news of Christianity is that we are integrated with God, not separated from God.

Christian life was never meant to be a life of alienation, of segregation, of disaffection. To me, that kind of life is antithetical to the joyous, abundant embrace of the gospel.

Reading the Bible with holism as our framework changes much about what we've long assumed the Bible to say. A few years ago a friend pointed me to a well-known section of the Bible, one that is often used to encourage Christians to circle the wagons in an effort to keep out the so-called dark forces of the world, Philippians 4:8–10. It reads, "Finally, brothers and sisters, whatever is true, whatever is noble, whatever is right, whatever is pure, whatever is lovely, whatever is admirable—if anything is excellent or praiseworthy—think about such things." Though we might not like to admit it, the theology of separation and distinction assumes that the "other" must be also be the "lesser." It assumes that there are far more bad "whatevers" than good ones and that it is only by limiting our engagement that we can follow God. But my friend sees it differently. He says, "I don't think that means we're suppose to limit our engagement through some elitist selection process of only the right things. I think it means we should be open to the 'whatever.'" This is a wonderful way to find the life of God—to look for the true and lovely and admirable in all places.

The theology of holism is a theology of invitation, of welcome, of God saying, "Look what I'm doing. Come and join me." The assumption is that God is present in all things, that we can find truth and nobility and righteousness and purity and loveliness in all things. In Romans 8:28, the apostle Paul writes about this Shema understanding: "And we know that in all things God works for the good of those who love him, who have been called according to his purpose." It's right there: "in *all* things." Not only in the special things. Not only in the holy things. Nothing is outside the reach and presence of God.

That goodness extends into our integration with other people. Because each of us is connected to God, we are connected to each other as well. Christians like to talk about community, yet the dualistic assumptions surrounding our theology make it almost impossible for us to experience true community. As long as we hold on to "us" and "them" categories of seeing the world, we live behind a barricade that prevents us from joining in with God and others in real and meaningful ways. And it doesn't really matter who we decide "them" is—the non-Christians, the sinners, the liberals, the conservatives, the Jews, the Catholics, that weird church on the other side of town. Division is division, no matter how righteous we want to make it sound.

> As long as we hold on to "us" and "them" categories of seeing the world, we live behind a barricade that prevents us from joining in with God and others in real and meaningful ways.

The apostle Paul was as clear as he could possibly be when we wrote, "Here there is no Gentile or Jew, circumcised or uncircumcised, barbarian, Scythian, slave or free, but Christ is all, and is in all."[4] Jesus, too, spoke often about the connections that exist among all people and between people and God. He said, "Because I live, you also will live. On that day you will realize that I am in my Father, and you are in me, and I am in you."[5]

For Jesus, the idea was not just that an individual would be in relationship with God and someday fly away to some other place but rather that people would find their purpose, their wholeness, their life through integration with God now and forever more. This is more than relational connection; it is full interconnection with God and Jesus, creation and humanity. This was, and is, extremely good news.

Embedded in the understanding of holism is the notion that we are not alone. We aren't just individuals plopped onto the planet to bide our time for seventy-odd years until the real action starts in heaven. We are part of a process. We are part of what others are doing and have been doing. And we are part of what God is doing and has been doing. Our lives matter not because of what will happen one day but because God has imbued life itself with profound significance.

I was talking about this idea with a friend, explaining this notion that God is about inviting us into life, that God is active in the process of eliminating from our lives whatever keeps us from living in rhythm with God. She responded by saying, "If Christianity isn't primarily about the promise of an afterlife for those who believe the truth, how would we ever convince someone to be Christian? What do we have to offer?" She was completely sincere, but I was taken aback. I don't mean to disparage her question—questions are what move us deeper into life with God. But for me, the idea of following a God who is in all things, who is inviting us to join in the work that is true and noble and pure, is so beautiful and so appealing that I can't imagine why we would offer anything else.

9

UP AND OUT

I have been aware of God my whole life. But it wasn't until I was sixteen, watching that Passion Play, that I finally knew God. I watched Jesus take on corrupt leaders, saw him defend the poor and broken, saw him speak for those who had no voice. Jesus, the Son of God, was touching and healing and standing up for the forgotten people. I was on board with this guy long before he hit the cross.

God was right there, working and moving and acting in the midst of the strangest, most compelling story I'd ever heard. God was alongside the tortured and beaten Jesus. God was on the side of people, bringing about goodness even in the midst of horror, betrayal, and struggle. God was inviting people to join in the redemption of it all. I didn't have the words for it at the time, but now I know that the Passion Play made sense to me because at its core, it was about a connected, compassionate God who was intimately involved in human life.

Like everyone else, I knew pain. I had been both the violated, lonely victim, and the oppressing, bullying offender in life. But in the Jesus story, I began to understand that God was the source of redemption for both the victim and the victimizer. God was about wholeness and healing and renewal—for the petty tax collector, for the spent prostitute, for the lonely teenager. God reached out a hand and I took hold.

This was the kind of story I wanted to live in. I had wanted to be part of what God was doing in the world, and now my sense of God's closeness, of God's invitation to be part of this life, was so powerful that it was all I could do not to climb out of my seat at the theater and run onto the stage to join God then and there. "Come on!" God was saying. "Look what I'm doing. Come and join me!"

But that feeling of stepping into a life of goodness and justice and redemption and participation was tested in the first ten minutes of my Christian faith. By the time I said, "Yes, I want to become a Christian," my hope of joining in with God's work in the world was replaced with the clear message that God wasn't all that interested in my help. In fact, God didn't really seem all that interested in human beings, period. God was in heaven and unreachable. Our human efforts to reach God, to touch God, were insufficient and really rather silly.

It was that little backstage booklet again. It began with the image of a canyon with a person on the left side and God on the right. The idea is that we are separated from God because of our sin, that God can't get to us and we can't get to God, no matter how we try. But then, with the turn of the page, a big cross appeared, dropped into the gap, and made a bridge. Of course, the bridge only appears once people have done the requisite bridge-building, which in this case came through proper belief and confession. But once the bridge is there, God and humanity can reach each other. Problem solved.

After what I had just seen and felt and followed on the stage, this seemed like an awfully strange illustration. During the play, it had been pretty clear to me that God was very busy on the human side of that "gap." It seemed like Jesus was declaring God to be on the side of people even before the crucifixion. It seemed like God wanted people to be free from sin, from pain, from sorrow.

To me, the story on the stage was one of God inviting people to join him, not people begging God to join them. But maybe I'd missed something. Maybe my assumption that God was involved in what Jesus was doing as he healed the lepers and befriended the lonely was way off. I wasn't sure what these backstage folks were suggesting. When I'd met them minutes earlier, I assumed they were in with the people who told the story on the stage, but maybe not. Maybe they hadn't seen what I'd just seen. Or maybe I had grossly misunderstood the play. I mean, what did I know about this story?

But there was something more problematic here. I wasn't just confused by the juxtaposition of this booklet and the play. I was confused by idea that there was a separation between God and me. My faith in God up to this point was shaped outside of a church environment, and even though I didn't have language for it and couldn't really articulate it, my faith was undeniably real and life-giving. The unformed faith that had been burgeoning in my soul all my life was genuine. It mattered to me. I believe it was the way God connected with me during those years. And it was based on my innate sense of God's closeness, on my longing to be connected to God, integrated with God, discovering God, living with God.

I had never felt separated from God. I didn't know much about God, but I had always been sure God was there, waiting for me. In fact, it was the clarity of God's care, the steadiness of God's presence in my life, that drew me into a life with God that night. I gave myself to a God who stood beside me, who would never abandon me. When God stayed with Jesus as he hung dying on the cross, I knew as surely as I have ever known anything that God would never leave me.

It was the clarity of God's care, the steadiness of God's presence in my life, that drew me into a life with God.

97

So it was really hard to make sense of this image of God on one side of a canyon and me supposedly on the other. The chasm itself was strange enough. But what was truly irreconcilable about this version was why God would be so stymied by the chasm. I understood that this was supposed to be a metaphor, but it sure didn't seem like a metaphor to the people leading me through the booklet. They talked about it literally, and in any case, it had an obvious effect on their notion of God. They described a God who, while loving me deeply, was distant, was hard to please, and needed to be appeased in order to participate in my life. They talked as though there truly was a gaping physical canyon between God and me and there was nothing either of us could do about it other than following the prescribed solution. All I could think was, *What an odd way to talk about the Creator of the universe—trapped on the far side of a canyon!*

I'm not sure I would have been interested in the Christian faith if the story on the stage had been about a removed God who needed to be placated with a blood offering before he was willing to cross the chasm and participate with humanity.

Maybe this image isn't troubling to others. And maybe it wouldn't have been troubling to me if I hadn't come to the Christian story with a story of my own. Maybe it wouldn't have bothered me if it hadn't been so different from the play I'd seen. But I'm not sure I would have been interested in the Christian faith if the story on the stage had been about a removed God who needed to be placated with a blood offering before he was willing to cross the chasm and participate with humanity.

As I was discipled in the Christian faith, I found that this God-of-the-Gap theology wasn't relegated to a one-off tract handed out in the back of a Jesus People Church. It was part of the common language and symbolism of the kind of Christianity I experienced. The Christian people I knew talked about God's transcendence, about God existing outside of our human categories and independent of our world. They used the image of royalty—God as the King of Kings—to elevate God to the highest possible position of authority and power. They talked about God's purity and holiness and otherness.

The God I learned about was, to be blunt, a God I wasn't sure I wanted to know. This God was perfect and removed. While this God loved humanity, God's love was conditional—it was only actualized for the right kind of follower. This God was opposed to most of humanity. This God was primarily concerned with the obedience of his subjects. Basically, this was the Greco-Roman hybrid God. I didn't know that at the time, and sadly, I too learned to talk about God up in heaven, not God in the world. I developed an understanding of God as the Perfect Mover, one never to be moved. I tried to think of God as those around me did—wholly other and nothing like me.

Even as I discipled others, I fought to make sense of this image of the up-and-out God. I waited for my lack of belief in this God to be replaced with a confident, fuller acceptance of the God of the Gap. But the more I learned of the "official" version of God, the more I wasn't interested in it. I found myself longing for the God I knew before I became a Christian—the one I'd whisper to at night, the one who made me feel less alone, the one who seemed to hold on to me when I was uncertain and in danger of losing my way.

I often got the sense that I wasn't the only one who felt this way. When more established Christians talked about God, I sometimes felt like they, too, bristled under the notion that God was up there, looking down on us. In times of crisis, I'd listen to fellow pastors quietly try to answer the question "Where is God?" Or hear pastors struggle to preach about finding a purpose in our time here on earth when the ultimate life is later, up in heaven with God. Older Christians who, I thought, had it all figured out would pray and plead for God to break into the world and fix all that was broken with a sense of sadness that they needed to ask. These moments were almost surreal; did these people feel the same disconnect I did? Did they sense the inadequacy of the up-and-out version of God? And if they did, didn't that mean we were all missing something?

Well, yeah.

Perhaps the best clue to how completely Greek Christianity eventually became is found in our imagination. When most Christians—at least most Western Christians—picture God, the image that comes to mind is of a majestic bearded white man sitting on a throne with a crown and a scepter. But that image doesn't come from the Bible. It is an image borrowed from Greek and Roman mythology. Our image of God as the all-powerful, removed, holy king is really much more influenced by Zeus and other gods than by the story of our faith. And when it comes to thinking about God, it turns out we borrowed a whole lot more than a statue from the Greeks.

Remember that in the first century there was an ideological clash between the Greek understanding of Plato's God as removed and unmoving and the intimate, hands-on Jewish God. Over time, the Greek view won out, and the Jewish understanding of God as creator, lover, leader, redeemer, judge, advocate, and mediator was recast by the Greek understanding. Between the third century and the fourteenth, these views were refined and codified into an entire system of belief, one that influenced science, astronomy, art, and pretty much everything else.

By the 1600s there were well-settled assumptions about the universe that translated into assumptions about the character of God. Primary among them was that everything in the universe was determined—settled and fixed. There was an established pattern for how all things worked and nothing was up for grabs. Isaac Newton took these well-known "facts" and developed the idea that the determined laws of the universe were as meaningful to theology as they were to science. So if the universe was well established and settled, it followed that the Creator was settled as well—that whole "the Creator made the creation so" business. Theology and science developed in light of the "known realities." A Christian confession written in 1646 put it this way:

Chapter III

Of God's Eternal Decree

I. God from all eternity, did, by the most wise and holy counsel of His own will, freely, and unchangeably ordain whatsoever comes to pass. . . .

II. Although God knows whatsoever may or can come to pass, upon all supposed conditions; yet hath he not decreed any thing because he foresaw it as future, as that which would come to pass, upon such conditions.

III. By the decree of God, for the manifestation of His glory, some men and angels are predestinated unto everlasting life; and others foreordained to everlasting death.

IV. These angels and men, thus predestinated, and foreordained, are particularly and unchangeably designed, and their number so certain and definite, that it cannot be either increased or diminished.[1]

No wonder people struggle to be Christian and believe that God lives with us and suffers with us. This confession tells us just the opposite: God plans everything that happens, good or bad. It is all God's doing.

Today, we know that the universe is far more beautiful, alive, and interactive than the imagination of the deterministic thinkers of the 1600s could allow for. It is best to not think of fixed laws that govern the universe but rather probabilities and possibilities that are inherent in the constantly changing world. Through discoveries about everything from the smallest particle to the expanding "multiverse" (formerly referred to as the universe), the notion of determinism has expired.

And that's a good thing. The deterministic version has never been able to tell the entire story. At the time, it may have been the best version available, but there is nothing admirable about keeping a notion alive through our religious expression that has no basis in reality. Because when someone like my friend Kara asks me, "Why didn't God make it stop?" I need to have an answer.

Kara's question is not an inquiry of the intellect but a pleading from the heart. It isn't a gotcha question meant to draw me into an argument. It is a cry of desperation, one I wish I could respond to in a way that would take away her pain for good.

Kara is the victim of sexual abuse. All abuse strikes at the heart of a person, but there is something about sexual abuse that seems to shatter the human spirit like nothing else. It creates a lifetime of insecurity and instability. Sexuality is an essential part of who we are as people, and when it is violated, the ripples roll through the entire psyche and into every relationship. It is an insidious evil. I know it. Kara knows it. And we both know God knows it.

I also know that Kara has asked this question hundreds of times. And I know that every time she hears a sermon or reads a Christian book or has a conversation about God, this question haunts her. Actually, that is a gentle way of saying it. Many of the victims of sexual abuse I've talked with are so angry with God that they can't even think about God, much less talk about God or show up at a church to "worship" God. Some are so confused about who they are and why these things happened to them that it has uprooted the very idea of certainty in their lives. Some are so beaten down that they give in to the devastating perspective of having nothing to lose. But at the core of all of these questions and uncertainties is a mistrust of God created in part by the perpetuation of the up-and-out, unpleasable, deterministic God.

Whenever I talk with people who are struggling to overcome abuse or addiction or any other kind of pain, I find that the only way to move forward is to put everything on the table and find a new starting point in talking about God. It doesn't do any good to work with the same assumptions about God that have continually led them to dead ends.

For a long time I found it incredibly frustrating to counsel people while trying to hold on to the Greek understanding of God. I didn't really believe it myself, but it was the official version of the holy and perfect God I'd been given, and I thought it was my job as a pastor to uphold it. But now I know that to talk about God in ways that are consistent with the full story of our faith, we need a view of God in which God is not up and out but down and in, fully here in the midst of our world, in the midst of everything.

This in the primary proclamation of Christianity: God is with us, God is in us, God surrounds us. The Hebrew name Immanuel means "God with us." The Jews believed in that God, the God who dwells among us. Theirs was an intimate understanding of God, one that suggests that God is fully present, fully involved, fully active. For many of us, this beautiful image of God is reserved for a few Sundays in December when we sing "Oh Come, Oh Come, Emmanuel" as a reminder of that long-ago event when God did come down and live with us for a few years. We've lost the hope, the connection, the intimacy that is so evident in the Jesus story.

The faith of people like my friend Kara, people for whom the up-and-out God is no longer sufficient, depends on our willingness to faithfully do as those who went before us did and tell the story of God in light of what we know to be true. In other words, we are called to tell a better story. A story of the down and in God.

10

DOWN AND IN

few months ago, I received this e-mail from a wonderful twenty-one-year-old in our church:

Hello Doug,

This is Danii, from solomons porch. used to have dreads, I dunno you will probably figure out who this is. Well I have planned on e-mailing you forever, I just never get around to it. I have wanted to say that I do not believe in the God of the Bible, and haven't for about a year and half, but I enjoy your community at Solomons porch and still go. But I have just been wondering as to what my role is or can't be in solomon's porch, I just feel a little awkward because you know, everyone meets for the same common interest or thought, and I don't really, well I meet for the people and community. Not with the commonality of belief or faith. But I don't know what the community is comfortable with, like me submitting art or helping out. I don't know, just wondering.

peace and love, Danii

I totally understood what she was saying. And after getting to know her better, I came to understand her perspective even more clearly. It wasn't that she didn't want to believe in God. Instead, she was having a hard time separating the God of the Bible from the dualistic, deterministic system she was told was mandatory belief. To her, they had become one and the same. She wanted a vibrant faith, one that honored participation and community and creativity in all people. But she'd been taught that unless her theology was right, unless her life and belief conformed to a model that would appease the unmovable

God, she was a failure as a Christian. That meant that all the people she knew from different backgrounds were also unable to live with God, and this seemed completely improbable and undesirable. As she described this understanding as the God of the Bible, I kept thinking, *I don't believe in that God either.* Her comments reminded me of a saying I heard once: "There are no pure atheists, but there are those who despise the God they have been taught to believe."

She'd been taught that unless her theology was right, unless her life and belief conformed to a model that would appease the unmovable God, she was a failure as a Christian.

Somehow so many Christians have become convinced that the up-and-out God is better and more holy than the down-and-in God. I've come to believe that much of this conviction is based on the limits of language. In some ways, language has always been at the root of our theological problems. I don't mean just the words we use but also the traditions and assumptions that express our beliefs. The way we worship, the way we read the Bible, the way we sing—these are all part of how we demonstrate what it means to be a Christian. Not only does our language help us speak to others, tell stories, and correct one another, but it also shows us how we're supposed to think.

My sense is that some of our up-and-out imagery for God has come about because it's so hard to find the right words for God without sounding trite or giving God too little credit. We believe we should have special words for God, that God surely needs to be described in ways that go beyond "good" and "kind" and "gracious." So we have held to the Greek worldview and used the language of royalty, of supremacy, of hierarchy. We have held tight to the Greek "omnis" for God—omnipotent, omnipresent, omniscient.

So any attempt to talk about God being close, involved, and integrated with humanity smacks of taking the deity right out of God, of turning God into little more than a really great guy. As if that weren't enough, the language of integration also brings with it concerns of glorifying humanity, of ignoring our supposed filth and sin and brokenness that goes along with the idea of the pure, unsullied God. Perhaps that's why Christians tend to get a little weirded out by the suggestion that God might be something other than up and out.

I became aware of this discomfort in seminary. We were talking about the all the "strange" biblical images of God. There are places where God is referred to as an eagle protecting her young,[1] as a nursing mother,[2] and as a hen gathering her chicks.[3] Our discussion was centered on why the writers would use such earthy, familiar language when referring to the Most High God. My professor explained that the writers were using the technique of anthropomorphism—giving human qualities to nonhuman entities. It was like my dad kissing his putter and saying, "That a girl," after making a tough putt.

We were taught that all those phrases in the Bible where God seems to be affected by human suffering or intimately involved in the lives of God's people were just poetic language that had nothing to do with the reality of God's nature. That nature, our professor explained, was summed up in the pre-scribed list of qualities of God—the omnis—and we shouldn't let the biblical narrative distract us from the truth about God. We were to understand these words as culturally bound tools used to describe God, not indications of the true nature of God. It was the down-and-in language that was thought of as culturally bound and not the up-and-out understanding.

This isn't just a seminarians' conversation. A few weeks ago Shelley and I were having dinner with some college friends, and one of them, Julie, asked me if I was familiar with a particular book she'd been hearing about. She had seen the author on *Oprah* and was bothered by the way he talked about God being "inside of us." She said, "I want God to be close to us, but we can't get too crazy with this idea of God being in us. God still needs to be God." Julie saw this conversation as the first step down a dangerous road of degodifying God, and she had no interest in going there.

This is the kind of thing I've heard my entire Christian life: "Be careful with this business about God being here and accessible and with us. It trivializes God." But that concern is based on what I find to be a tragically misdirected under-standing of God, one that serves no one well, least of all the church. A God who is distant and removed is not better than a God who is engaged and caring. A God who is immovable is not better than a God who is participating. A God who is up and out can never outdo a God who is down and in. Saying that God participates in creation does not trivialize God; it's a faithful understanding of the God of the Bible.

This problem runs so deep in our Christian culture that it has been the undoing of countless people of faith. In fact, I find this misrepresentation of God to be among the most damaging, dangerous theological missteps in the Christian tradition.

I can't tell you the number of conversations I've had with lifelong Christians who hit a crisis in life and find themselves confronted with the depth of their belief in the removed God. These are the people who give up on their faith when their marriages fail or their children die or their lives just don't seem to work out. They haven't been given a picture of God as one who cares, who listens, sustains, cradles, cries and is right there with them all the time.

Many of us live in this in-between place, working to make sense of the God we have been told about in the face of the God we hoped to find. My friend Amy had a similar experience with this distant God after the birth of her first child. She told me, "I was talking with one of my friends about how paranoid I felt as a mom, how I couldn't stop thinking about all the dangers out there and how frightening it felt to be responsible for this little person. My friend said, 'You have to give your child over to God. Once you trust God with your baby, you won't be so anxious anymore.' I really wanted that to be true, but I found that I didn't trust God one bit! Every day you hear about some child being abused or abducted or killed in a car accident or dying from some bizarre disease. I'd grown up with a faith where God was all-powerful and would break out the vengeance on whoever he wanted, whenever he wanted. So in my mind all those tragic things were God's doing either by intent or neglect. God was the *last* one I'd trust with my baby."

For Amy, this conversation led to the realization of how deeply she held the image of the up-and-out, impossible-to-please God. She says, "I had this belief that while God was in ultimate control and God might be forgiving, God never forgets. I could never be repentant enough for this God. I just knew that one day the other shoe would drop and something I loved—my child—would be taken from me. It sounds ridiculous to say it out loud, but that's truly what I felt." Years later, Amy still struggles to believe in a God who loves her completely, who lives life with her, a God who values her and her participation in the world. She admits, "Even though I know better, that powerful, vengeful God who can barely stand to look at me is so profoundly part of my Christian heritage that if something were to happen to one of my children, I'd still believe it was because God wanted to punish me for my sins."

Personal faith isn't the only part of Christian life to crumble under the force of the up-and-out God. It creates fallout that infiltrates every other aspect of belief as well. As with all language, the language of the God of the Gap belies assumptions about sin and humanity, forgiveness and grace, life and death.

Obviously, the chasm in the tract illustration was meant to represent sin and the way it keeps us from God. But that assumes not only that sin separates us from God but also that sin separates God from us. And that simply isn't the case. I don't believe that sin is

The God of the Bible is active and involved in the lives of the just and the unjust, the good and the bad, the saints and the sinners. The God of the Bible is actively bringing about the healing, forgiveness, and completion of all the world.

more powerful than God. I don't believe that God is stymied by sin. The God of the Bible is active and involved in the lives of the just and the unjust, the good and the bad, the saints and the sinners. The God of the Bible is actively bringing about the healing, forgiveness, and completion of all the world.

Certainly God was with me even when I was an "unrepentant sinner." The sin in my life may have kept me from fully living into life with God, but it wasn't keeping God away from me. And I can't imagine any Christian trying to convince me otherwise. We know that's just not true. Yet the God-of-the-Gap theology stubbornly persists in so many of us.

There are those who believe that moving away from the God-of-the-Gap theology means ignoring or being soft on sin. They worry that any language in which God likes us and wants to be with us prevents us from recognizing our sinfulness. I'll say more about sin in a later chapter, but it's worth touching on it here. I believe that there are better ways to talk about sin than with the language of distance. I think that sin is best described as disintegration.

We all know what it feels like to be in relationships that are pulling apart. We all know families who live in the same house, eat at the same table, and share the same genes yet live in conflict with one another and have little of what passes for relationship. We all know people who struggle to love themselves, who can't seem to find peace with who they are and where life is taking them. These aren't problems of distance but problems of integration. They are the result of people feeling at odds with themselves and others. Enmity doesn't require distance.

Although I had a clear sense of God's closeness before I became a Christian, I also had a clear sense of the disconnection between us. I knew that there was a life with God that was in no way similar to mine. I knew that I was living in way that hurt the efforts of God. There was strife but not distance. In fact, it was the closeness of God that caused the strife. God was so embedded in the world that my lifestyle kept bumping into the good things of God. And every time that happened, I felt the sting of not knowing how to hook into those good things.

My conversion was the beginning of a new way of living, a new connection with God. God hadn't been waiting for me to do something before God was willing to get involved in my life. God had been involved all along. The disconnection ended not when God decided I was righteous enough or clean enough or enough of a believer to cross the bridge but when I saw what it looked like to live life with God and understood the invitation to join in.

And thank God for that. If we buy into the Greek version of God, and therefore the Greek version of sin and humanity, we are left with terrible consequences. There's an internal logic here that few of us talk about but that many of us live by all the same. If we believe that God is reachable only when we are fully changed, we're stuck with an afterlife-focused faith.

The theology at play here is one in which our sins are removed from our permanent record. The death and resurrection of Christ doesn't stop our sinning; it just makes it so that our sins stop counting against us. That means that when we die and go to heaven, we are allowed in because our sins have been erased. But until then we are incomplete, imperfect, flawed, broken—pick your metaphor. The gap might be bridged by the cross, but it never really closes.

The idea that God's plan is for us to bide our time in this miserable life until God decides it's time for us to escape to heaven certainly doesn't paint God in a very appealing light. Even the notion that we are to live righteously out of gratitude for the promise of salvation does little to propel many of us into living joyously here and now. Really, with its focus on our unworthiness and God's separateness, it promotes just the opposite kind of life. It suggests that we're lucky God doesn't smite us all with one stroke of a mighty hand, that it would be beyond audacious for us to believe God has any use for us at all. Now that's a belief system that will suck the joy of living right out of you.

And what is the gospel if not a message of joy, a message of hope? When our theology strips us of joy and hope, something has gone horribly wrong. In April 2007, the week when a student at Virginia Tech shot and killed thirty-two other people before killing himself, I was flying home from a conference. Somewhere over the farmlands of Ohio, I was thinking about the people I'd met at the conference and their dreams of changing their churches for the better. Then I started thinking about the thirty-three families who would bury their loved ones in the days to come, the young people who would be forever changed by the loss of their friends and professors. Underneath all of this was my fear of airplanes. (I fly a lot, but on almost every flight, I still look out the window at the ground some four miles below and think, *This sucker could nose-dive at any minute*.) This mix of fear, despair, and hope was swirling around in my head when a song written by my friend Ben started playing on my iPod. Ben sang:

Peaceful God, hopeful God
Somehow, always we have known

We're not alone.
The kingdom is near.
Living the Mystery, undoing fear.
We're not alone.

We often sing this song at our church, and my eyes well up nearly every time I hear it. It speaks to the essence of faith, to the way God is present in the bleak landscape

When our theology strips us of joy and hope, something has gone horribly wrong.

that hides seeds about to burst through the earth, in the lives shortened and damaged but never lived in vain, in the deep-seated belief that we can be agents of God's goodness in the world. It speaks even in my fear of crashing, which is undone by the peace offered in the present, active love of God.

I don't want to follow a faith based in fear. I find it far more compelling—and far more biblical—to live a life in which we are called to join with God, to be like God, to live the Jesus story. From the moment I became a Christian,

I wanted to be in the midst of the story proclaiming "Emmanuel"—God has come near.

I wanted to be part of a life in which we say, "Your will be done on earth as it is in heaven." I wanted to be in the midst of the story proclaiming "Emmanuel"—God is near.

11

WONDERFULLY MADE

It was the ultimate in junior high bus abuse. I was starting sixth grade, which meant a new school. It also meant sharing the yellow tub of torture with ninth graders. I didn't know all the subtleties of bus politics, but I knew enough not to sit in the back—that was the domain of the ninth graders. And I knew enough not to claim a front seat—that was the place for kids who wanted to talk to the bus driver or had to keep track of their band instruments.

On the first day of school, I was scared spitless. One of the drawbacks of being a big kid—in sixth grade I was six feet tall and weighed 160 pounds—was that everyone assumed I could keep up with the older kids. I was pretty good at faking cool, but deep inside I knew those ninth graders were way out of my league. So I took my place just in front of the "love seat," so dubbed because it was the seat above the wheel well, and anyone sitting there was teased for being "in love" with the other person in the seat. At least that had been the story on the elementary school bus. But that was when the bus was innocent, when the worst thing we could think to do was tie a GI Joe to the back of the bus so it would trail behind us, tormenting the neighborhood dogs along the way.

On the junior high bus, cruelty was reserved for the riders.

The back of the bus was ruled by the Kane boys. They were a tough lot. Earlier that summer I'd seen Davey Kane take a header off his bike onto a road where a crew had just laid a topcoat of fresh gravel. Rocks embedded in his face and he barely cried. I was almost in tears just looking at him. Cripes, I get the shivers just writing about it! That was one tough kid.

But he wasn't the mean one. The mean one was Kevin.

It took only three stops that first morning for Kevin to hit his stride. As the door opened, I heard Kevin say, "Get ready." I looked around, trying to figure out what he was preparing for. A girl walked on to the bus. And it started:

"Didi Dorf sucks royal! Didi Dorf sucks royal! Didi Dorf sucks royal!"

An unremarkable girl turned down the aisle, eyes on the rubber rug, shoulders hunched, as though by disappearing into herself she could make them stop. She sank into the second seat as the boys in the back repeated their chant. It must have gone on for less than a minute, but if felt like a lifetime.

I didn't know her, and I had no idea what she had done to become the recipient of such cruelty. From her appearance it looked like she had a pretty tough life—she often came to the bus looking disheveled and on one occasion showed up still in her pajamas. (I assumed she had woken up late and her parents—or whoever she lived with—made her get on the bus anyway. It was moments like this that I felt deep love for my parents.) I didn't know if Dorf was her full last name or a shortened mocking of it. But it didn't matter. The barbs were headed straight for her, and she couldn't do anything to stop them.

This happened every day during the first week. And each day more people joined in—the boys and the girls, the older kids and the younger kids. I wasn't one of them, but that's not necessarily something to be proud of. It wasn't an act of bravery on my part to slide down in my seat and hope Kevin never set his sights on me. It wasn't enough to resist the crowd; Didi needed someone to protect her from their violence. But as a twelve-year-old, I didn't have it in me to throw myself between the abuser and his victim.

Finally on Friday, just as it seemed like the entire bus was about to take part in this verbal abuse choir, the bus driver stopped the bus, stood up, and turned around. "Stop it!" he scolded. "Why do you keep saying that to this poor girl?"

Kevin, in an act befitting his brash rudeness, replied without missing a beat, "Because she does!"

The driver turned to Didi and bent down to say something to her. I like to believe he was telling her that they were wrong. That she didn't suck. That she was valuable and important. That she was beautiful and wonderful and had world-changing potential because she was made in the very image of God. I like to believe he protected her with the truth.

The driver must have done something more than that, because Kevin wasn't on the bus for a week, and when he returned, there was no more chanting. I don't know what became of Didi Dorf, but wherever she is, I hope she's experienced enough love to override Kevin's taunts. As for Kevin, I hope he's experienced enough love to find forgiveness for the pain he caused a young girl.

This is a story that doesn't need explaining. No one hears it and wonders why Kevin was in the wrong. No one questions whether Didi really did "suck royal." Because none of us believe she did. None of us believe she deserved to be treated this way. As Christians, we believe that Didi is a precious child of God who is "fearfully and wonderfully made," just like the Bible says. Even those who don't hold to any religious understanding of humanity are stirred by stories like this—you don't have to believe in God to believe that it's wrong to be cruel to another human being. We have an instinctive belief that there is a goodness in all human beings that needs to be protected and preserved. There is an age-old Christian understanding of each human being as *imago dei* (Latin for "the image of God"). There is even a Christian tradition in which humans are thought of as icons through which we can see and connect to God.

Yet those of us who learned a particular version of Christianity were told another story of humanity. When I became a Christian, I found out that I wasn't all that wonderful and never had been. In fact, I was a pretty big disappointment. God may have created me, but I was deeply flawed, so flawed, in fact, that God couldn't even look at me without seeing all my dirty sins and failures. And there was no getting out of this mess on my own. It was as deeply ingrained in me as my DNA. It was passed on to me at birth as part of the human condition.

On the upside, I wasn't alone in my sinful state—all of humanity was there with me, a big mass of us, sucking royal. Jesus could bridge the gap between God and me, but that didn't change the rotten state of my essential being. Until I got to heaven, I would just have to accept that I was a broken, wicked sinner. That message came from a lot of people, but it didn't seem to come from the God I read about in the Bible, the one who so loved the world, the one who made human beings the penultimate achievement in all of creation, the one who wanted to love and be loved by these very same people.

The biblical story is one that inspires us to live out God's love for us as we interact with one another. It's the one that reminds us that people are good and kind and creative. It's the one where we are moved to protect each other and care for each other and show compassion to each other. It's the one that tells how we are created to partner with God for the redemption and restoration of all the world.

But that story has been papered over by a version of the creation story I like to call "From Very Good to Really, Really Bad." Other people call it "The Fall." It goes like this:

God created the earth and everything in it. And it was good.

Day after day the creation was good.

God created human beings and it was very good.

The thing is it didn't stay that way for long. Not long after they were created, Adam and Eve disobeyed God and ate what should not have been eaten. This sin had great consequence; it was not just disobedience. It changed all that very good-ness and plunged Adam and Eve into a depraved, fallen state. This fallen state somehow changed the nature of humanity. The original status was lost and replaced by original sin and a debased version of humanity that was then passed from parent to child like a genetic disease.

Every Christian has heard some version of this story of the fall. The technical aspects of it might be up for grabs, but the basic ideology—that human beings are inherently depraved and broken and that's why our perfect God cannot be in a relationship with us until we are fixed up—remains the same.

It might seem like I'm exaggerating to make a point, but honestly, I'm understating the case. The official version proclaimed by the many varieties of Christian faith through the ages states that human beings start their lives as sinners who are not just bad but enemies of God. Back in the 1640s the Church of Scotland tried its hand at articulating a view of humanity in order to teach people the doctrines of the church. The result is the Westminster Confession of Faith. Here's that version of the story:

I. Our first parents, being seduced by the subtlety and temptations of Satan, sinned in eating the forbidden fruit.

II. By this sin they fell from their original righteousness and communion with God, and so became dead in sin, and wholly defiled in all the parts and faculties of soul and body.

III. They being the root of all mankind, the guilt of this sin was imputed, and the same death in sin and corrupted nature conveyed to all their posterity, descending from them by original generation.

IV. From this original corruption, whereby we are utterly indisposed, disabled, and made opposite to all good, and wholly inclined to all evil, do proceed all actual transgressions.

V. This corruption of nature, during this life, doth remain in those that are regenerated; and although it be through Christ pardoned and mortified, yet both itself, and all the motions thereof, are truly and properly sin.

VI. Every sin, both original and actual, being a transgression of the righteous law of God, and contrary thereunto, doth, in its own nature, bring guilt upon the sinner, whereby he is bound over to the wrath of God, and curse of the law, and so made subject to death, with all miseries spiritual, temporal, and eternal.[1]

It's pretty clear that it's a sorry fate to be human. And as much as we'd like to believe we have moved beyond such extreme theology, this explanation has held so firmly that many churches still uses this catechism in their teaching.

I'm not trying to pick on the Presbyterians. The Lutheran Church has its own version of this story dating back to 1530. It goes like this:

It is also taught among us that since the fall of Adam all men who are born according to the course of nature are conceived and born in sin. That is, all men are full of evil lust and inclinations from their mothers' wombs and are unable by nature to have true fear of God and true faith in God. Moreover, this inborn sickness and hereditary sin is truly sin and condemns to the eternal wrath of God all those who are not born again through Baptism and the Holy Spirit.[2]

In 1801, the Anglicans and Episcopalians decided to say it like this:

Original sin standeth not in the following of Adam, but it is the fault and corruption of the Nature of every man, that naturally is engendered of the offspring of Adam; whereby man is very far gone from original righteousness, and is of his own nature inclined to evil, so that the flesh lusteth always contrary to the Spirit; and therefore in every person born into this world, it deserveth God's wrath and damnation. And this infection of nature doth remain, yea in them that are regenerated; whereby the lust of the flesh, is not subject to the Law of God. And although there is no condemnation for them that believe and are baptized; yet the Apostle doth confess, that concupiscence and lust hath of itself the nature of sin.[3]

Franklin Graham, who has taken over the ministry of his father, Billy, and is quite different from his father, was quoted in *USA Today* in 2006 as saying, "Man's heart is the same everywhere. It's evil. It's wicked. The human soul is a putrid sore of greed, lust, and pride."[4]

It's one thing to recite these confessions and statements in a Sunday school class. It's a very different thing to live out a theology of inherent depravity (that humans start out lacking anything good). We can say we believe that humanity is evil and depraved and that we enter the world this way. But I don't think this fits the Christian story, nor do many of us truly hold to it. I mean, I've never heard of someone walking the halls of a maternity ward and saying, "Oh, what a collection we have here of dirty, rotten, little sinners who are separate from God and only capable of evil!" Rather, the impulse is to say, "What wondrous, beautiful miracles." Or to borrow a phrase from the creation story, "It is very good." New life just doesn't seem to fit with this notion of inherent depravity.

New life just doesn't seem to fit with this notion of inherent depravity.

And a good thing it doesn't. If we really lived out a theology of depravity, we would have a very different society. One could argue that the logic of every person being born depraved and living as a sinner until being released from sin at the point of death makes infertility a sign of God's kindness—one less child will have to live with the scourge of sin. It makes the death of a loved one a blessing—that sister or brother or child or parent is no longer imprisoned in sin. It makes the birth of a child a cause for sadness and sorrow as another miserable sinner comes into being—that baby is one more problem added to an already dark world. It means Didi Dorf really did suck.

The disconnect between what I was taught about the human condition and what I knew and believed to be true finally made sense when I realized that the theology of depravity was yet another hand-me-down from the fifth century and the church's efforts to create a clear Greek-Christian hybrid. Theologians like Augustine were responding to the continuing changes in both Christianity and the broader culture. Their ideas were birthed in environments that called for particular explanations of sin and salvation.

By this time, Christianity was no longer a fringe religion practiced in a few fishing villages—under Constantine, it had become a mainstream religion in the Roman Empire. The faithful, in turn, sought to codify Christianity in order to give compelling reasons for the existence of the church. Naturally, trying to get this still-burgeoning faith to fit into an efficient and effective package was no easy task. People like Augustine, Irenaeus, and Chrysostom did their best to create a systematic approach to Christianity that would make it understandable and accessible.

The doctrine of inherent depravity was, in part, Augustine's effort to explain the necessity of participating in the state religion—since the church was now official, people could join as a part of their citizenship. Those most committed to the faith felt compelled to help others see that the church was important in its own right, that involvement could be more than just a civic obligation. So the explanation went something like this:

All people have a need only the church can fill.

People are born with a problem—depravity.

That problem can only be rectified by God.

But the thing was, people couldn't get to God because they were inherently evil. So they needed a go-between. The only solution was Jesus, who fixed the problem of the original sin inheritance. And Jesus could only be accessed through the church, which administered the sacrament of baptism. It was baptism as a means of grace that freed the individual from the ramifications of depravity. It was the continuous playing out of these ideas that led the Lutheran confession to include the phrase "this inborn sickness and hereditary sin is truly sin and condemns to the eternal wrath of God all those who are not born again through Baptism and the Holy Spirit."

This issue became especially important in regard to the spiritual state of children. For Augustine, sin was passed on through sexual intercourse. That meant babies, though loved by God, were in a state of damnation from the moment of conception. They needed the grace of God applied to them through baptism, which could only be administered by the church. In a time of high infant mortality rates, this was a pretty good motivator.

Of course, Augustine and company weren't pulling all of this out from under their tunics. Augustine's doctrine of depravity was based on a particular linguistic and cultural reading of certain passages of the Bible, which by this time had been translated from Hebrew and Greek into Latin. Specifically, he based it on passages such as Psalm 51:5; Ezekiel 18:4; John 8:44; Romans 2:5, 12; Romans 8:20–23; 1 Corinthians 15:22; Galatians 1:3–5; Galatians 4:8–9; Colossians 1:13; Hebrews 9:27; and 1 John 5:19. I don't believe for a minute that Augustine was trying to pull one over on the faithful or that he had anything but the most faith-filled intentions as he worked out this doctrine. But the starting point of his view of humanity was a cultural assumption about duality and separation from God. He tried to provide a Christian answer to this dilemma. Like all of us (including me, with my theology of integration), Augustine read Scripture through a cultural lens, one that led him to certain conclusions about God, sin, and humanity.

At the same time, it's no accident that the people explaining the problem had a lock on the solution. It's the number one rule in sales: create a problem only you can see and then offer a solution that only you can provide.

For all that went into it, this view is a culturally particular theology. And it's important for us to remember that theologies are contextual explanations of various aspects of faith. They aren't meant to stand in for truth or our common story. Instead, they act like adapters that allow our presuppositions and experiences to fit with the story of God. They are not the story itself. They are, at best, an explanation of the story for a given place and time.

By definition, theologies are always limited and biased. And it's a good thing they are. Good theology makes sense of things that don't seem to make sense. But the things that don't make sense change with each generation, with each location. The Greco-Roman world had a terrible time making their assumptions of human frailty and limitation gel with the story that humans are created in the image of God. So the theology of depravity made sense to people who held a view of humans as being something less than God had intended. It answered significant questions about the church's role in saving people, which had real benefit in a world where conversion to the faith was now an act of citizenship. However, the rationale for this view of humanity has expired, and so ought the theology that grew out of it.

There is a better story, and it's being told every day, but not necessarily by those who claim to speak for God. This hit me one Sunday morning while I was watching *Meet the Press*. A commercial came on for GE Healthcare. It's the one that begins with a tight close-up of a baby. He has an "everybaby" look to him, with no clearly defined ethnicity. He's just plain cute. Then the narration begins: "Welcome to the earth. It's a great time to be alive." The narrator goes on to talk about all that might be possible in this little guy's lifetime—driving a car powered by water, that sort of thing. The narration continues with this message of hopeful potential as the scene cuts to a wide shot of the baby. He is in a carrier on his mother's back facing another baby who is in a carrier on his father's back. As the two babies reach toward each other and give a high-five, the narrator concludes, "This just might be the best time to be alive. Welcome to the earth."

I was struck by how different this message was from the one I feared was being heard in churches that same morning. Someone flipping channels at home would hear a message that said, "This is a wonderful world, and we're so glad you're here." But what was happening in Sunday school rooms and church sanctuaries around the country? Were the people there hearing that the world is in deep trouble, that things have never been as bad as they are right now and are only getting worse? Were they being told they were sinners who were only contributing to this misery? Was someone telling them that if they wanted to find the source of darkness in the world, they should start with a look in the mirror?

That's why we need to tell that better story, the story that lets us know that we are created in the image of God, as partners and collaborators with God. This very well might be the best time to be alive, not because of new health care efforts but because we are here—you and me—and we are to join with God in the world. We live in a time of hope because we are God's people and God is a God of possibilities, of potential, of goodness. When we give up on ourselves, on our inherent connection to this God who created us to live in partnership with him, then we give up on God as well.

> We need to tell that better story, the story that lets us know that we are created in the image of God, as partners and collaborators with God.

My hope is that we never lose sight of what it means to be created in the image of God.

When I was in sixth grade, I didn't know how to stand up to the bullies at the back of the bus. But the deeper I go in my Christianity, the more I feel compelled to be the bus driver. I can't sit by as someone tells me, my children, my friends, that they suck, that they are evil to the core. And I certainly can't stand to have that perverted message be the imposter of the gospel of Jesus. I need to be someone who steps between the abusive accusations and the victim. I need to be someone who whispers the truth.

12

SAME AS IT EVER WAS

I'm writing in a coffee shop filled with all kinds of people, including a mother with a new baby. A few minutes ago, a three-year-old boy came in with his mom. Immediately, the boy zeroed in on the baby. He has made his way over to the couch where her carrier is perched and is straining on his tiptoes, trying to touch the baby. Rushing to follow him, his mother says, "Ask the baby's mom if you can touch her." She keeps telling him to ask, but the boy doesn't seem to hear her—he just continues his reaching and stretching. From where I'm sitting, I can see his eyes getting brighter and brighter as his hand gets closer and closer. His mom stays on message, but this is no time for decorum—there's a baby to touch!

Finally, just as the baby's mom says, "Yes, it's OK," his little hand reaches the prize. He gently rubs the baby's sweet, downy head, and his whole body is overtaken with joy. He giggles and squeaks and shivers with the thrill of it all.

To him this little girl is wonderful. She is a treasure. He can see the goodness of life in her. It isn't just her softness that appeals to him—he's completely ignored the velvet couch they are sitting on. No, he wants *her*. She is alive. She is like him. This little guy who can barely talk—barely listen—can see that this baby is precious. She is wonderful. She is full of God's life.

The little boy doesn't care that her skin is pale and his is dark. He doesn't care if she might one day have a different set of beliefs than his. Life may hold friendship or enmity between these two, but that doesn't matter; for now he wants nothing more than to reach out, touch, and share the joy of living.

This little boy has yet to learn that the baby he's touching is something separate, something apart from himself. All he knows is that he and the baby are meant to be touching. They are meant to be near each other. They are meant to be connected. His innate understanding and desire to relate to this baby is part of his makeup. And it's part of ours too. We are all created for connection, created to love and be loved. We are created to live in partnership and harmony with one another and with God. That's the way it's been from the beginning.

> **We are all created for connection, created to love and be loved. We are created to live in partnership and harmony with one another and with God.**

The creation story of the Bible has long been used not as a precise description of what happened but as a teaching narrative by which the followers of God can tell the broad story of faith. After years of hearing the depravity version of the creation story—and sensing that there was something askew with it—it was tremendously helpful when I took a fresh look at Genesis and found that the story actually goes like this:

God created the earth and everything in it. And it was good.

Day after day the creation was good.

God created human beings in the very likeness of God and it was very good.

Everything was just the way it ought to be. God and humans were in full partnership. God walked in the garden with these human partners. Adam and Eve were called to do as God did—name what exists and create new things. Their lives were whole, and they lived in harmony with God.

> Then God said, "Let us make human beings in our image, in our likeness, so that they may rule over the fish in the sea and the birds in the sky, over the livestock and all the wild animals, and over all the creatures that move along the ground." So God created human beings in his own image, in the image of God he created them; male and female he created them. God blessed them and said to them, "Be fruitful and increase in number; fill the earth and subdue it. Rule over the fish in the sea and the birds in the sky and over every living creature that moves on the ground."[1]

Life was good in the garden. We learn that Adam and Eve were naked, yet they felt no shame.[2] They were at peace with God, with each other, and with themselves. Yet even in the midst of this "garden of perfection" there were limits. There were foods that ought not be eaten and things that ought not be done.

> The LORD God took the man and put him in the Garden of Eden to work it and take care of it. And the LORD God commanded the man, "You are free to eat from any tree in the garden; but you must not eat from the tree of the knowledge of good and evil, for when you eat of it you will certainly die."[3]

That's when the trouble began.

Now the serpent was more crafty than any of the wild animals the LORD God had made. He said to the woman, "Did God really say, 'You must not eat from any tree in the garden'?" The woman said to the serpent, "We may eat fruit from the trees in the garden, but God did say, 'You must not eat fruit from the tree that is in the middle of the garden, and you must not touch it, or you will die.'"

"You will not certainly die," the serpent said to the woman. "For God knows that when you eat of it your eyes will be opened, and you will be like God, knowing good and evil."

When the woman saw that the fruit of the tree was good for food and pleasing to the eye, and also desirable for gaining wisdom, she took some and ate it. She also gave some to her husband, who was with her, and he ate it. Then the eyes of both of them were opened, and they realized they were naked; so they sewed fig leaves together and made coverings for themselves.

Then the man and his wife heard the sound of the LORD God as he was walking in the garden in the cool of the day, and they hid from the LORD God among the trees of the garden. But the LORD God called to the man, "Where are you?"

He answered, "I heard you in the garden, and I was afraid because I was naked; so I hid."

And he said, "Who told you that you were naked? Have you eaten from the tree that I commanded you not to eat from?"[4]

Their state of being did not change; their DNA didn't change; they were as naked as ever, but suddenly they saw it as a problem. They knew they had acted against God, and they felt the loss of the harmony they once shared. They were embarrassed, and they hid from God and blamed each other. They didn't want God to know what they had done, how they had lost track of what God was doing.

God felt the loss as well. God was hurt. God wondered why they had done this. There were consequences to their actions, serious consequences. Adam and Eve were created for seamless life with God, but they had stepped away from that life. As a result, their lives would be full of struggle and strife. Birth would bring pain. The ground would not only give life but also take it. When they were in sync with God, they had only life. But being out of synch with God would bring death.

Yet even in the midst of this struggle, Adam and Eve partnered with God. They still cared for the land as they were created to do. They still brought children into the world. They were even part of the plan for all the strife to end and death to lose its power. Their story goes on, with the whole of creation living in fits and starts of participation with God.

This story never suggests that the sin of Adam and Eve sends them into a state of depravity. There is nothing in the story that tells us that God steps over to the other side of some great chasm once Eve bites down on that fruit. Certainly there is sin, but the result of sin is a change in our relationship with God and with others, not a change in the basic makeup of humanity. The creation story tells us that although we are capable of tragic missteps, God's hope and desire is for us to continue to join in to the good things God is doing in the world. We are still capable of living as the children of God.

Once the story of Adam and Eve is freed from the confines of out-of-date theology, it points us to a more accurate view of humanity: we are created in the image of God to be God's partners in the world. This is what it means to be human.

Some people say that the primary purpose of humans is to "glorify God and enjoy him forever." Although many people will

We are created in the image of God to be God's partners in the world. This is what it means to be human.

find life in that call, to me it seems a bit shortsighted. It suggests that the human endeavor is basically a vertical arrangement—we exist for God's pleasure and, through God, our own. I'm just not sure that's the whole story.

The Genesis account of creation doesn't mention anything about glorifying God in the sense of offering God praise and worship. Instead, God's relationship with humanity began when God created Adam and put him to work in the garden. God wanted Adam there. God wanted Eve there. They *were* the glory of God. God wanted humanity to participate in what God was doing—creating, naming, tending—to be co-laborers with God. The biblical story says that the "chief end of man" is to live in harmony with God as partners in love and work—loving and working with God, loving and working with one another, and loving and working with all of creation.

That truth, then, ought to become central to the way we live with one another. When we believe that people are inherently godly rather than inherently depraved, it follows that all people have worth, that all people have God-inspired goodness to offer. There is no separate, lower status for those who are not Christians and no special, upgraded status for those who are. Every person, in every nation, of every religion, of every social and economic group, of every color and persuasion is created in God's image. Every person is created to partner with God.

And every person is created to love and be loved. This isn't something we have to be taught. We don't have to learn how to be attracted to other people. In fact, one of the signs of something not being whole and healthy in a child is the failure to form **The human need for emotional connection is so natural that its absence is considered abnormal. We instinctively care for other people.** emotional and social bonds with other people. The human need for emotional connection is so natural that its absence is considered abnormal. We instinctively care for other people.

So often it is in times of crisis that we see the very best in people. When the Interstate 35W bridge collapsed into the Mississippi River in 2007, the national news started talking about infrastructure. But here in Minnesota, we also told stories of the remarkable ways people risked their lives for one another, the way people comforted one another, the way people valued the lives of strangers and frightened children. This is more than just hardy Minnesota gumption at work; it is basic human goodness. We know how to love the way we know how to breathe.

Of course, we don't always live out that love. As much as I want to see the face of God in all people, I must admit that it is incredibly hard for me. I often find it easier to see what's wrong with other people rather than the goodness God has put in them.

Here's an ugly confession: I have a hard time being around people with disabilities. It is a truly shameful part of my character. I envy people like my daughter, Michon, and my son Chico, who not only never miss a beat when they're with people whose bodies don't quite work right but seek out ways to serve and befriend the disabled. Not me. I get nervous. I get stuck. I don't know what to say. I'm not even sure what words to use—handicapped? disabled? impaired? limited? challenged?

I have created a few coping strategies. Whenever I'm about to meet a person with a disability, I try to remind myself that this is a person who deserves care and respect as one created in the image of God. I try really hard not to focus on the parts of the body that are different from mine but to find the humanity of the person. I try to see what's working instead of what isn't. I do what I can to look the person in the eye and talk as I would to anyone else. For the most part, looking a person in the eye and seeing his or her humanity has been an important and effective first step.

But I don't always have the luxury of prep time. And that's when I come face to face with my awful bigotry toward those with disabilities.

Not long ago I was speaking at a weekend event. The dining room at the conference center was set up with tables for eight. As I walked through the buffet, I scanned the room for open seats. I noticed a few at a nearby table. I walked over, but as I got closer, I saw that the chair I was headed for was next to a woman in a wheelchair. It was too late to backtrack—I'd made eye contact, and the people at the table had that "come-and-sit-with-us!" look on their faces.

I started running through my coping mantra: *Look her in the eyes. Don't think about the wheelchair. Act normal.* I sat down and introduced myself to everyone. So far, so good. The woman in the chair, Claire, was smart and funny and full of energy. I enjoyed talking to her so much that we ended up sitting together at the rest of the sessions, making wisecracks from the back row.

But during lunch I was so nervous that I worked a little too hard at maintaining eye contact and didn't really pay attention to the new people who came to join our table. As they sat down, I took a drink of my water and then looked up to say hello. I'm pretty sure everyone could hear me as I choked on my water and muttered a little "Oh, dear God!" The woman sitting across from me had only one eye.

Granted, she was wearing a patch, but it was black and stark, and I felt my stomach sink. *What am I going to do now?* I didn't know what to say, so I turned hard to my left and quickly started a conversation with the woman beside me. I was in a panic here, grasping for something to talk about. Seeing a company logo on her tote bag, I asked if she worked for that company—safe territory, right? Wrong.

"No," she said. "I'm a pastor. The bag belongs to my wife, but she let me use it for the weekend."

A wife? She had a wife?

I sat there with a woman in a wheelchair on my right, a one-eyed woman across from me, and a gay clergywoman (and all the politics that entailed) on my left. I had hit the trifecta of awkwardness.

It didn't help that I was in the middle of writing about the wonder and beauty of humanity for this book. I was overwhelmed by my hypocrisy. I was so ashamed that I couldn't see beyond the things that made Claire and the one-eyed woman (whose name I never even asked for) different from me. I couldn't see them for who they were, only what they were. The more I thought about it, the more I felt like I was the one with the disability. I was the one who wasn't able to live right in the world.

I walked out of the dining room feeling like a total loser. It was almost enough to make me want to blame my weakness on all of humanity.

Thankfully, there was still time to get over my weird issues and move forward into love and friendship. I never did cross paths with the one-eyed woman again, but after Claire showed me the cool things she could do with her high-tech motorized chair and we spent more time together, I told her I hoped we'd see each other again soon. And I secretly hoped she would help me grow out of my discomfort with wheelchairs. Our friendship continues to this day. The tote bag pastor and I said good-bye with a hug and a promise to hold on to our growing friendship, which, to my benefit, has indeed happened.

I wonder if what's true for me is true for a lot of us: My tendency to see the struggles in other people comes at my expense. It is not at all the best way to live with my fellow human beings.

For years I thought that the depravity view was the only truly Christian perspective on humanity. Then I read about the Celtic Christians who proclaimed humans as those who possess the light of God within them. That light might brighten or dim as a person lives well with God or moves away from God, but the light is never extinguished.

I learned of Orthodox Christianity, which developed without the full acceptance of sin as depravity and saw humans as the very image of God. Although I never wanted to blindly grab onto the Celtic or Orthodox version as the final resting place—they have limitations of their own—I did find great solace in the realization that the Christian story wasn't written by just one group of people with one set of culturally bound perspectives.

> I find great solace in the realization that the Christian story wasn't written by just one group of people with one set of culturally bound perspectives.

I also find great solace in the fact that the Bible itself tells a far different story of humanity. The whole of the Bible points to the beauty of humanity and God's continued involvement with us. From Adam and Eve through Revelation, God loves and participates with human beings.

Like so many religious people today, there was a tendency among the Jewish followers of Jesus in the first century to see two kinds of people: those who were chosen and blessed by God ("us") and everyone else ("them"). But Jesus called his followers to erase these distinctions between the righteous and the unrighteous (and I'm sure he would call us to do the same). Jesus said:

> You have heard that it was said, "Love your neighbor and hate your enemy." But I tell you, love your enemies and pray for those who persecute you, that you may be

children of your Father in heaven. He causes his sun to rise on the evil and the good, and sends rain on the righteous and the unrighteous. If you love those who love you, what reward will you get? Are not even the tax collectors doing that? And if you greet only your own people, what are you doing more than others? Do not even pagans do that? Be perfect, therefore, as your heavenly Father is perfect.[5]

It couldn't be clearer: we are to live a life that follows God's lead—be perfect as your heavenly Father is perfect.

All of creation is God's, and all of creation is called to join in with God. We are not to love some people and not others—God makes no distinction, and neither should we. The chief end of all humanity, of all creation, is to live like God. Yes, people turn away from God. Throughout the Bible, people commit horrible acts of violence and injustice against one another. But in every case, God is present, actively bringing people back to God and back to the agenda God has for the world. God's heart breaks every time people live outside of God's hopes for them. God seeks to do all that is necessary to help people love justice, seek mercy, and walk humbly with God.

I know there are times when God's activity recorded in the Bible—and in our world right now—seems extreme to us, even cruel, but I'm convinced that that's our limited perspective at work. God is still working at redeeming the entire world. Throughout the Bible, there are declarations from God, reminders from the gospel writers, and admonitions from the apostles that alert us to the ongoing nature of God's activity in the world:

> "Do I take any pleasure in the death of the wicked? declares the Sovereign LORD. Rather, am I not pleased when they turn from their ways and live?"[6]

> "For I take no pleasure in the death of anyone, declares the Sovereign LORD. Repent and live."[7]

> "For God did not send his Son into the world to condemn the world, but to save the world through him."[8]

> "That is why we labor and strive, because we have put our hope in the living God, who is the Savior of all the people, and especially of those who believe."[9]

> "The Lord is not slow in keeping his promise, as some understand slowness. Instead he is patient with you, not wanting anyone to perish, but everyone to come to repentance."[10]

God loves this world and all who are in it. God not only loves humanity but created humanity as the ideal partner for bringing about all that God desires for the world. We are not working against our lesser nature when we seek to live with God; on the contrary, we are living as we were created. The joy of this proper understanding is that we no longer have to feel ashamed of our humanity. It is not a sin to be alive.

13

THERE GOES THE JUDGE

My family loves to cook. Well, I should say Shelley loves to cook, and she gets the kids in on the act whenever possible. I, on the other hand, don't care much for the kitchen apart from what ends up on the table. I don't like the shopping, the cleaning, or the conversation about how the cook found the perfect mushrooms or should have added a bit more basil to the sauce. I just like to eat.

But I do have the occasional moment of team spirit. A few weeks before Christmas in 2001, I decided to do something nice for the foodies in my house. I have watched just enough Food Network to know how important it is to have really good knives and to keep them nice and sharp. The point was literally driven home for me when I cut my hand while slicing a tomato. Apparently, a sharp knife cuts neatly and cleanly, whereas a dull knife slips around and jams into the knuckle with enough force to leave a guy gasping.

Anyway, I decided to take our big, dull, knuckle-stabbing chef's knife to the knife store to get it professionally sharpened as a surprise for Shelley. I decided to sneak the knife out of the house one day while Shelley was supposed to be at work. I was in the kitchen, coat on, knife in hand, looking for a bag to put it in when Shelley came in—she had come back home to get something. Quick-thinking guy that I am, I hid the knife in the pocket of my big winter coat. I made up some story about why I was leaving and rushed out the door.

I drove to the store where we bought the knife. They told me they didn't sharpen knives and sent me to the cutlery store at our local mall. As I pulled into the mall parking lot, I got a call from my friend Tim in Kansas City. We had been trying to talk for weeks, so I put in my earpiece and took the call. By the time I walked to the cutlery store, Tim and I were deep in conversation. I wandered over to the middle of the mall, near the escalators, to finish the call.

I was in classic multitasking mode. Talking on the phone, pacing about a bit, thinking about the knife, watching the clock to make sure I'd get home before Shelley did. Before long, I pulled the knife out of my pocket and started absent-mindedly running my thumb along the edge of the blade to see how dull it was. After a few minutes, I noticed a security guard from the mall walking around and keeping his eye on me. At first I didn't think much of it—I had other things going on.

But after a while, I could feel the guy's eyes piercing the back of my head. I said to Tim, "Hang on a second. I'm going to say something to the security guard who keeps looking at me." I turned around to find that the security guard had been replaced by a plain-clothes police officer, one who had his gun drawn and pointed at my face.

He shouted, "Drop the knife! Get on the ground, right now!"

I was terrified. I really thought this guy was going to shoot me. He had a crazy-eyed look, the kind I guess police get when they have to pull their guns in the mall to apprehend a long-haired, six-foot-six, knife-wielding assailant wearing a big hooded coat and talking to himself.

I kept thinking, *Just do what he says and he won't shoot you.* In what seemed like mere seconds, seven other officers showed up with their hands on their guns. I could hear Tim in my earpiece asking, "Dude, what is going on? Are you OK?" I wasn't about to say anything, so Tim started yelling,

"I'm staying on the line. What is going on? Should I call the police?"

I let go of the knife and dropped to my knees. The officer kicked the knife away and shouted, "Lay on your stomach and put your hands behind your back!" I did what he said. The officer then put his knee between my shoulder blades, cuffed me tightly, and told me to roll on my back. I tried to do it, but it's not easy to roll when you're in handcuffs and pressed up against a glass partition by the escalator.

The officer yelled at me again as he grabbed me by my hood and lifted my chest off the ground. As he pounded me, face first, back into the floor, I could hear Tim shouting, "Are you being mugged? What's happening to you?" The officer then yanked me to the sitting position. That's when he noticed the earpiece.

He ripped it out of my ear and said, "What is this?"

"It's my cell phone," I said as calmly as I could.

"Who were you talking to?" he demanded.

"Tim. In Kansas City."

Then the questions really started:

"What are you doing carrying a knife in the mall?"

"Getting it sharpened at the cutlery store."

"Can you prove that?"

How do you prove something you haven't done yet? I gave it my best shot. "Well," I said, "I was just at the Williams-Sonoma store across the street. They told me to come here."

Turning to another officer, my keeper said, "Can you call and check that?" Then he looked back at me with pure distain in his eyes. "Did it ever dawn on you not to bring an open knife into the mall three months after the terrorist attacks?" he asked.

"Uh, well, um, I guess not, but I wanted to surprise my wife and then she walked in the kitchen and . . ."

"What do you do for a living?"

"Uh, well, I'm a pastor."

"Seriously?"

"Yeah."

"Oh, boy."

After ten minutes of questions and phone calls, the officer walked me into the cutlery store and said to the clerk, "Sharpen this guy's knife and give him a bag." With that he walked away.

The clerk said, "Um, well, we don't sharpen knives at this store, but here's a bag."

Perfect.

Once I got back to my car, I was overcome with the emotion of it all. I was still incredibly scared and shaking. And I was embarrassed. I was mad at myself for being stupid and at the officer for using what seemed to me to be excessive force. For the first time in my life, I felt like the police and I were not on the same side.

I had always felt good about the police. Even when I was "arrested" in fourth grade for shooting my fellow Village Terrace resident Storm Hultgren in the leg with my BB gun, I believed the police were there to "serve and protect." But that afternoon driving back from the mall, I felt like a criminal and a victim at the same time. I passed a squad car on the way and thought, "Screw you."

When I got home, I told the story to my family. They laughed like crazy, but I was getting madder by the minute. I realized that I'd been stupid, that I'd been in the wrong, but this whole thing had gotten out of control.

I know the officer was just doing his job. And I understood his motives a bit more when I learned from my friend Tony, who works as a police chaplain, that the officer was working in the mall as part of sting operation. Apparently, the restroom on the floor just below where I'd been standing was a meeting place for men hooking up with sex partners they'd found online. The officer probably thought I was there to hurt someone. Instead, I was just a dumb guy trying to finish a phone call and do something thoughtful for my wife. But when it comes to the legal system, there's only a right side and a wrong side. And no one likes being on the wrong side.

Unfortunately, religious life is not so different, particularly when it comes to sin. For centuries, Christians have used the language of the legal system to define sin and its consequences. God is the judge, God's commandments are the law, and breaking the law brings on God's judgment in the form of death and damnation. There is a debt to be paid, so Jesus comes along and pays it on our behalf. This blood atonement is the restitution laid out for our crimes. For many Christians, this is more than just a metaphorical way of understanding sin; it is a synopsis of the gospel.

Early in my faith I learned a popular analogy for this judicial model of sin and salvation that goes like this: Imagine you stole something and got arrested for it. Your day in court comes, and you are convicted. At your sentencing hearing, the judge declares that you must pay a $2,500 fine or spend forty-five days in jail. You obviously don't have the money, or you wouldn't have stolen in the first place. So you say to the judge, "I cannot pay this fine, so I will have to serve the time."

At this point the judge stands up and takes off his robe. You realize the judge is your dad.

He takes out his checkbook, writes a check for $2,500, and places it on the table in front of you. He turns around, puts his robe back on, sits behind the bench, and says, "Now what are you going to do? Are you going to pay the fine with the payment provided, or are you going to pay the penalty with your life?"

This story represents the way I was taught to understand sin—as an offense against God, one that must be paid with our lives. And naturally, given that this judicial model is normally coupled with the view of inherent depravity, no one escapes God's judgment. The upside of this view is that we are all in the same boat. In theory, it doesn't matter who we are or how much power or money we have; everyone is equal under the law.

This, of course, is a necessary element of a workable system of justice. The absence of this kind of equal protection and equal accountability is the primary mark of a corrupt government. The legal system under which we live here in the United States does seem to be the best model for keeping order and peace in a society. But I'm not convinced it's the best model for understanding the way sin affects the relationship between God and humanity.

For starters, it's a model that hamstrings God. In the legal system, even the judge is beholden to the law. The law is the guiding force, not the judge.

Shelley and I are trying to open a natural-health café in a house we own. This involves changing the zoning of the building, a process that's long, complicated, and full of legalities and regulations. In one of the many meetings I've been required to attend, I worked with the head of zoning for Minneapolis and the city councilman for our neighborhood. They are both very supportive of our effort, and they're working hard to help us get the approvals we need. But they can only do so much.

The city councilman expressed his frustration with the local ordinances, saying, "In situations like this, it becomes clear that sometimes the laws that are designed to benefit the area actually prevent the kinds of things we would like to see in the neighborhood." The zoning guy agreed. But what could they do? The law is the law, and they have to live with it. As true as this might be for council members and codes and ordinances, it's unsettling to think of God stuck in this same conundrum.

Even Jesus saw the absurdity of this idea. When his disciples were questioned for picking grain on the Sabbath, Jesus said, "The Sabbath was made for people, not people for the Sabbath. So the Son of Man is Lord even of the Sabbath."[1] Jesus regularly debunks the notion that the law is the beginning and end of faithfulness. He does this when he makes his "you have heard it said . . . but I say to you" statements about how we are to relate to God and one another. During his famous Sermon on the Mount, Jesus said, "You have heard that it was said, 'Eye for eye, and tooth for tooth.' But I tell you, do not resist an evil person. If anyone slaps you on the right cheek, turn to them the other cheek also. And if anyone wants to sue you and take your shirt, hand over your coat as well. If anyone forces you to go one mile, go with them two miles. Give to the one who asks you, and do not turn away from the one who wants to borrow from you."[2] He said, "You have heard that it was said, 'Love your neighbor and hate your enemy.' But I tell you, love your enemies and pray for those who persecute you, that you may be children of your Father in heaven. He causes his sun to rise on the evil and the good, and sends rain on the righteous and the unrighteous. If you love those who love you, what reward will you get? Are not even the tax collectors doing that? And if you greet only your own people, what are you doing more than others? Do not even pagans do that? Be perfect, therefore, as your heavenly Father is perfect.[3]

Jesus is suggesting another way for us to live in relationship with God, one that has nothing to do with the legal model.

The story of the gospel is so much better than the legal model suggests. It tells us that we are created as God's partners, not God's enemies. Sin does a lot of damage to that partnership—it disables us, it discourages us, it disturbs us—but it never destroys the bond that exists between God and humanity.

> The story of the gospel is so much better than the legal model suggests. It tells us that we are created as God's partners, not God's enemies.

The legal approach recasts our ideas about God, justice, redemption, and salvation. These ideas create tension for plenty of good-hearted Christians who say things like "My sister is stuck in an awful abusive marriage and I wish I could tell her to get out and get help. But I know the Bible says divorce is wrong. I just don't know what to do for her." These questions get even harder when people struggle with the idea that God is confined to the limits of the law. They'll say, "I had an abortion when I was younger. I've asked for forgiveness, but I know I broke God's law, and I think God is still angry with me for disobeying him."

In the judicial model, God must judge us according to the law. But God is allowed to show us mercy as long as the punishment for our wrongdoing is carried out. So God, who is evidently powerless to do otherwise, must offer Jesus as a blood sacrifice in our place. Yes, it breaks God's heart to do it, but what choice does God have? The law is the law.

The helpless-God version of the story is problematic, but at least God comes across as likable. He's akin to the family court judge who doesn't want to return the child to his abusive parents but has no choice because of the law. But the even more troubling version that many have heard, the one that makes us shiver when we hear it, gives us God as the angry judge who will exact his payment at any cost.

In this view, God is not a softy but rather a hard-nosed, immovable, infallible judge who cannot abide defiance of the law. And boy, did we defy it. When Adam and Eve broke God's law in the garden, they offended and angered God. So heinous was their crime that their punishment extended to all of humanity for all time. The antidote to this situation is the crucifixion of the Incarnate Son of God because only the suffering and death of an equally infinite and infallible being could ever satisfy the infinite offense of the infinitely dishonored God and assuage his wrath. Yikes!

Even when someone uses a variation of the judicial model, the situation is the same: the judicial model of sin puts the law at the center of the story. In doing so, love, grace, mercy, compassion, goodness, and even God become minor players that must be subject to the law. The gospel itself becomes less about God and more about the sin problem.

It also makes sin a catchall excuse for every human failing. Every longing, every weakness, every mistake is equated with sin. This is part of the reason the Greeks had to suggest that **When sin is the center of the story, it skews our understanding of everything else.** God was unchanging—change was driven by a lack of something, a longing for something, and God could lack for nothing. When sin is the center of the story, it skews our understanding of everything else.

Yet this sin-centric story has hung on for centuries. At this point in the book it should come as no surprise that this alteration in the core message of the gospel came as a result of the early church's efforts to create a compelling, cohesive story that would make sense in the Greek worldview. The concept of innate depravity did more than help the citizens of Rome see the need for the church. The problem of sin created a need for God.

The Romans weren't the only ones to buy into this line of thought. I've had people say to me, "I need God in my life because I am a desperate sinner. Without God, I am nothing but a hopeless wreck." The desperation created by the theology of depravity makes it impossible for us to imagine life without God. Maybe the end result is fine—I can't imagine life without God either—but the path these folks follow to get there is riddled with problems.

This theology of depravity is based on a story Christians have been telling for centuries, the one where we are inherently evil to the core and in need of a savior who can rescue us from our inbred evil nature. Now I need to be careful here because I am by no means suggesting that we don't need Jesus or that sin isn't real—in a few pages I'm going to expend an enormous amount of effort explaining why I believe Jesus is crucial to my faith. But I think we've got the whole story backward.

Rather than starting with Jesus and following his story, we've started with sin—more specifically, with our theologized assumptions about the way sin separates us from God. We've started with a problem that wasn't a problem until someone decided to make it one. As a result, Jesus is little more than a means to an end. In his book *The Divine Conspiracy,* Dallas Willard calls this "sin-management faith." He says it makes us "vampire Christians" who need Jesus for his blood and not much else.[4]

The judicial model of sin is not a biblical view of God, humanity, or even sin itself. The doctrine of depravity was created to address a specific problem. Until then, sin wasn't seen as something that changed the ontological state of humanity. It wasn't something that created an unbridgeable gap between God and us. But as the doctrine of depravity took hold over the centuries that followed, it changed the way people understood the church. And it changed the way Christians understood what it meant to be Christian. Faith became a means of salvation, a way to extinguish the fire of evil that was thought to burn in us all. Rather than being the hope-filled, forward-leaning life with God that Jesus talked about, Christianity too often became a pessimistic, evil-obsessed religion of sin management.

Matthew, Mark, Luke, and John each tell the story of Jesus with an emphasis on his relationship with the outsiders—the unfaithful, the broken-down, the sinners. Jesus continually calls these people to join in with God. He rarely talks about the sin problem outside of calling people to be freed from it. Instead, his is a message of what could be—a life of peace, justice, healing, hope. Take this parable Jesus used to explain what it means to be part of the kingdom of God:

> "There was a man who had two sons. He went to the first and said, 'Son, go and work today in the vineyard.' 'I will not,' he answered, but later he changed his mind and went. Then the father went to the other son and said the same thing. He answered, 'I will, sir,' but he did not go. Which of the two did what his father wanted?"
>
> "The first," they answered.
>
> Jesus said to them, "Truly I tell you, the tax collectors and the prostitutes are entering the kingdom of God ahead of you. For John came to you to show you the way of righteousness, and you did not believe him, but the tax collectors and the prostitutes did. And even after you saw this, you did not repent and believe him."[5]

The tax collectors and prostitutes (the ultimate sinners in those days) were not the wrong kind of people to live with God. They were the ones who did what God would have them do. They aligned their lives with the things of God, with the work of God. Jesus was less interested in where they'd come from than in where they were heading.

That's not to say that sin didn't matter to Jesus. It mattered greatly. But it mattered for reasons that are vastly different from the reasons sin has mattered to the church for so long. Jesus cared about the sin in people's lives because sin kept them from being fully invested in life with God. Sin mattered because it was less than what God wanted for humanity.

Jesus cared about the sin in people's lives because sin kept them from being fully invested in life with God. Sin mattered because it was less than what God wanted for humanity.

Sin matters because it kills and destroys all of creation, not because it breaks some code. Most of us instinctively know when something is destructive or out of step with creation. We don't have to be told when something is sin; we know when life is not in harmony with God. This is what Paul argues at the start of his letter to the church in Rome: "For since the creation of the world God's invisible qualities—his eternal power and divine nature—have been clearly seen, being understood from what has been made, so that people are without excuse."[6]

We don't need anyone to tell us that child abuse is sin. We don't need anyone to tell us that rape is sin. We don't need anyone to tell us that hate is sin. We know that such acts are not in line with what it means to live like God. We know we are better than that. The disharmony is recognizable in light of what we know should be there instead.

We feel the awfulness of sin because we can envision life without it. Frustration comes when we can see a possibility but can't make it reality. People don't get frustrated when they, say, can't dematerialize and move through space instantly; we don't see that as a reality to which we should aspire. We don't feel frustrated because we can't create a meal with a snap of our fingers like Samantha on *Bewitched*; we don't expect life to work that way. We grow frustrated and angry with sin because we know we are capable of better. We cry out over the brokenness around us because we know that's not the way it should be.

Sin isn't a legal problem with God; it's a relationship problem with us. In the garden, Adam and Eve were perfectly integrated with God. But when they ate from the tree, they acted outside their partnership with God and began to experience the disintegration of their relationship with God. And that's what sin is—disintegration. We were created for integration, partnering, connection with God. Sin irritates; it destabilizes. It causes us to come unraveled from the life we have with God.

Judgment, then, is not complete when God's anger is satisfied but when our integration with God is re-created. In our culture we tend to think of justice being brought about when a guilty person gets the proper consequence. But justice isn't about paying someone back or even making people pay for what they did. Justice is best understood as redemption or reconciliation. The Old Testament uses the Hebrew word *karem* in many of the passages about God's judgment. It means "healing" or "remaking" or "returning something to its intended purpose." God's justice is the restoring of things to the way they ought to be. We are intended to live with God and to live like God. Sin derails that effort. When the disintegration stops and integration arrives, God's judgment is complete.

The idea that God is a removed judge sitting behind a bench doling out punishment for our crimes minimizes sin. Sin is more destructive to humanity and to God than any judicial matter. Sin is not just a wrong done by those who are predisposed to do such things. Sin is not something that offends God's sensibilities. Sin destabilizes humanity and pushes us to the brink of total destruction. We don't need punishment, but *karem*—healing redemption. We need to be re-created, freed, born again, and made whole. This is the gospel's good news about sin. We are invited to live free from sin and destruction, to seek lives lived in harmony with God.

14

BEHIND BLUE EYES

I am in the people professions. In my work as a pastor, in my speaking, and in the property management business I own, I interact with all sorts of people in all sorts of situations. I have been in funeral homes, morgues, hospitals, and living rooms with people in the midst of the hardest times of life. I have participated in and been caught in the middle of hate-filled fights. I have held the hands of people taking their last breath. I have gotten involved in people's finances and tried to help them keep their homes. I have cleaned up other people's vomit and fecal matter. Countless times I have had people lie right to my face. I have been assaulted and violated and felt unbearable pain. I have wept with the victims of rape, abuse, and murder. I have listened to confessions that made me physically sick. In the midst of all this pain, failure, and cruelty, I find it impossible to think of these situations as legal issues.

These are not stories of broken rules. They are stories of lives falling apart, of people in dire states of total disintegration. The legal model of sin management is a fairly easy way to make sense of sin. But it ignores the real complexity of sin and its ramifications. Sin destroys and kills. Sin rips people apart from what they could be. It taints our relationships with God and with others. It twists our sense of ourselves.

In no way am I suggesting that believing people are wondrous creations made to participate with God means life is sinless. It is not. Life is riddled with the impact of sin in all its ugliness. But sin is not the definer of life; it's the destroyer of life. In fact, anything that destroys life is sin. Frankly, I am suggesting that *more* things are sin, not *fewer,* for anything that derails life is sin. But also embedded in my thinking is an important distinction missing from the legal model: hope.

Sure, sin is everywhere, but it is not the end of the game. When we have a proper understanding of sin, we are able to acknowledge it without a complicated system of blaming our ancestors or humanity or assuming that God is put off by it. No, when sin is active, we must deal with it; the good news is that we can.

> When sin is active, we must deal with it; the good news is that we can.

This was the thinking of the Hebrew community in the Old Testament. This can come as a shock to those Christians who are so used to hearing that Jesus is the solution to sin that they assume the remedy started with the death of Jesus. The Jewish tradition tells us otherwise.

In our church community, Deborah, who was raised Jewish, often leads us in festivals of Jewish origin to help us more deeply understand our Christian faith. Each fall she leads us in a practice of Yom Kippur, the Day of Atonement. Deborah reminds us that in the book of Leviticus the nation of Israel was called to a day of atonement every year. She goes through the details of the prescription given to Aaron and Moses and makes the obvious connections to the Jesus story: the scapegoat, the blood being shed, the confession to one another and to God, and the declaration of freedom from sin.

Deborah tells us each year that the Jews would celebrate the Day of Atonement by gathering lint from their pockets, every little corner of them. She invites us to do the same. Then we write confessions on pieces of paper or pick up leaves to represent each sin and walk to the edge of a stream. As we drop our leaves and papers into the stream, we read from the Psalms:

> For as high as the heavens are above the earth, so great is his love for those who fear him; as far as the east is from the west, so far has he removed our transgressions from us. As a father has compassion on his children, so the LORD has compassion on those who fear him.[1]

Deborah then reminds us that just as the water carries our words away, God takes our sin from us. As far as far can be, sin is removed, taken, gone. Yes, sin exists, and when we find it, we should get rid of it.

This understanding of sin allows us to look at the world with eyes wide open, to see the sin that seems to entrap so many, and still proclaim that life will win over death. Sin is anything that "dis-integrates" us from God. This includes sins committed intentionally and accidentally. It includes sins that are systemic and those that are occasional. It includes sins perpetrated by humans and sins brought on by other parts of creation. But sin is not the point. We do not live life to manage sin. We live life to join with God, and when sin comes knocking at the door or crouches in the corner or rises from within us, we seek to do away with it. We flee from it. We eradicate it. We plot against it. Sin is not what makes us human. Sin destroys our humanity and all the rest of creation.

We do not live life to manage sin. We live life to join with God.

When I talk about this disintegration understanding of sin, I find that many people have the same question: If sin isn't the result of an inherent flaw in us, if we aren't born depraved, then why do we sin? It's a fair question, but I think it pulls the conversation backward.

Laura, who is part of our church and one of the finest people I know, was sitting with my editor and me while we were talking about the content of this chapter. Laura had her little baby, Alice, on her lap, and we were being all goo-goo over her in the middle of our conversation. We were talking about how the story of fallenness would suggest that Alice, even in her sweet little four-month-old body, was capable of only evil because she had not been baptized, but that Laura, who had been baptized and was an active believer in Jesus, would be thought of as the one who was less influenced by sin.

It made no sense. Since we are all parents, we agreed that rather than seeing our babies as full of evil and ourselves as freed from sin and growing in goodness, it seemed to work the other way. "Truth be told," she said, "we all just hope we don't screw the kid up with all our sin." We agreed that we were the ones deeply affected by the sin that comes as we live our lives, and we hope that our children can avoid it whenever possible.

This is the opposite of what the classical view would hold, that people start rotten and get better if the right formula is applied. It is much more the case that the systems, hurts, and patterns of our world create disharmony with God and one another. It is life that creates illness and sin.

Disintegration has a way of building up, as if it gets in us and eats away at us. And at times we do sin's bidding on purpose. We even seek it out. As hard as it is to admit, we are often the ones who run from what God desires for our lives. Or we are the ones who put up roadblocks that keep us from following God. And then there are times when we are the victims of other people's sin.

Sometimes it is our bodies, not our conscious decisions, that do us in. Work being done by neurologists, biologists, and chemists show that many of the problems that have long been classified as sin have their cause in our biology. There are times when our sin comes from our development as human beings because our development has gone wrong.

Brian, a pastor friend of mine, once put words to this. He said, "I used to call most everything people did wrong a moral or spiritual failure. But now I know that if you get many of those same people on the proper diet or medication, their 'sin' seems to go away." He wasn't saying that every problem could be solved by a healthy meal or a pill. Instead, he was acknowledging the role of our bodies and brains in our struggle to live well with God. This is exemplified as we see Jesus in the gospels healing the broken, the sick, the diseased as a sign of forgiveness of sin.

Regardless of how it comes—whether through our habits and systems, our intentions or the doing of others, or our bodies and biology—we live with sin. But we also live with the possibility of freedom from sin.

We live with sin. But we also live with the possibility of freedom from sin.

The good news in all this is that sin never gets the last word. We can live our lives in a collective way, so the systems that cause disharmony with God can be changed. We can change the patterns wired into us from our families and create new ways of relating and being. Our bodies can experience healing. In other words, we can be born-again, new creations.

The National Institute of Mental Health has found that nearly 30 percent of the population struggles with some kind of mental illness.[2] That statistic certainly holds true for me. For whatever reason, my life includes all kinds of people who suffer from varying degrees of mental illness. The more I've learned about mental illness, the more it has given me a framework for understanding sin that is so much more helpful and biblical than the judicial model.

For a long time my connections with those suffering from mental illness were primarily professional. But to live in a family with someone who struggles deeply to live at peace with himself is a whole other thing. Adopting our boys has greatly expanded my sympathy and understanding of what it's like to be unable to live an integrated life.

Our son Chico lives with the effects not only of a birth mother whose consumption of alcohol changed her baby's developing brain structure but also of spending his early years with parents and grandparents who treated him badly. These traumas have created tremendous problems for Chico. In addition to the struggles that are common to everyone, Chico has to work with a broken body in order to be the kind of person he wants to be.

For Chico, his "perfect storm" of issues culminate in what has been categorized as post-traumatic stress disorder, fetal alcohol affect, intermittent explosive disorder, and reactive attachment disorder. Those are the technical diagnoses. The real-life play-out is that he is a victim of his own brain activity and chemistry. His body and his desires live at odds with each other. What he wants to do and how his body responds are at times so disintegrated that he is tormented by his own personhood.

Chico's desire is to live a complete, good, kind, whole life. But his body is broken. It is damaged. It is not whole. And because we are created as holistic, integrated beings, when the body is broken, the will, the spirit, and the mind are all broken as well.

On countless occasions these issues have manifested in explosions of anger and violence to the point where Shelley and I have had to physically restrain him for hours at a time. We have learned how to administer a safety hold designed to keep us and Chico safe. There are times when these episodes last for two hours. They involve Chico hitting, screaming, biting, and calling us names. They are filled with emotion on both sides and they are totally exhausting.

In the midst of these episodes, we try to remind Chico—and ourselves—that this will pass and his body will be healed. We try to remind ourselves that while we will lay out consequences for Chico's behavior, we love Chico and plan to do all we can to help him find wholeness. Still, it is incredibly difficult.

In every way I can think of, this is just what sin is: the disintegration of what is normal and desired. If Shelley and I understood Chico's issues as acts of pure willfulness, we would be forever frustrated and would see him as the enemy who is causing trouble. If we saw his condition as unchangeable human fallenness, we would simply pity him. But we believe there is healing for Chico. We believe it because we've seen it.

Chico has received significant help from people who understand how he can change his brain function through therapy and diet. Shelley and I have done extensive work with Chico through the Family Attachment Center of Minnesota, which has helped us use narrative therapy to bring about amazing changes in his neurological pathways and his behavior. Coupled with the work of the wonderfully dedicated special education professionals at his school, these treatments have helped Chico not just live with but overcome some of the many obstacles he faces every day.

We all struggle with a similar kind of internal conflict between what we want to do and what we actually do. This struggle is not based on a legal model but on a health and integration model. This distinction between those who can be helped by healing and those who need to be punished by the judicial system is crucial. When societies deal with mental health issues through the legal system, they usually end up doing far more damage than good. And so it goes with faith. The legal model drives us into places of despair and self-loathing. It creates distance between us and God. It makes us afraid of God and suspicious of others. But when we think of sin as disintegration, as the unraveling of life and goodness, we hold on to the hope that there is healing and integration, that a life can be woven back together from the threads that remain.

Last summer we were in the midst of one of our annual long road trips in our Grand Caravan. We have a set seating arrangement—me driving, Shelley riding shotgun. Michon sits behind me, and Taylor crams his long body into the seat behind Shelley. Ruben and Chico sit in the third row, a perfect fit for their shorter-than-the-average-Pagitt legs.

We were listening to a random selection of music when the song "Behind Blue Eyes" by the Who came on. The song ends with the line "No one knows what it's like to be the bad man, to be the sad man, behind blue eyes." Chico said, mostly to himself but loud enough for us all to hear, "I do."

We all broke out in laughter. And so did Chico. We weren't laughing at him. We all know Chico, have all suffered with Chico, have all longed for Chico to have a better life. So our laughter came from our intimate understanding that indeed, Chico knows what it's like. Shelley said, "You sure do, Chico; you sure do. But that's not all there is, buddy. That's not all."

Shelley was saying that we are more than our misdeeds. We are more than our struggles. Certainly, life and growth are still coming, but being people who don't always live up to our human- **But we are called by the belief that we can live up to who we really are—the wonderful, valued, image-bearers of God.** ity doesn't mean we suck. Chico doesn't do these things because he is awful; he does them because he is still healing and becoming. Yes, Chico, all of us know what it is like the to be the sad and the bad. But we are called by the belief that we can live up to who we really are—the wonderful, valued, image-bearers of God.

15

THE JEW I NEVER KNEW

J esus was a Jew, you know."

"Nuh-uh," I responded eloquently. "He was a Christian."

The thought continued in my head, *like me now*.

Within days of my experience at the Passion Play, I was oozing my new faith and eagerly talking about it with anyone who would listen. That's how I ended up in a school stairwell with a girl I sort of knew, bumbling my way through the first of many awkward conversations about Jesus.

She stood there looking at me like I had missed out on the most basic component of faith, as if the Jewishness of Jesus was one of the top three things a new Christian should know about the guy. My mind quickly rifled through everything I'd learned over the weekend: God loves me. Check. I'm standing at the edge of some weird canyon. Check. Jesus is my new best friend. Double check. Jesus was a Jew? Uh, what?

I walked away from the stairwell in silence, completely thrown by what she'd just said. Even with my extremely limited understanding of the Christian faith, I understood that Christianity and Judaism were two distinct religions. I had a bunch of Jewish friends, and I'd been to my share of bar mitzvahs, and nobody ever mentioned Jesus. My Jewish friends went to synagogue on Friday nights and Saturday mornings, while my Catholic friends were out of commission all day Sunday. No overlap, no common ground, just two religions doing their own thing. Her "Jesus theory" just had to be wrong.

What really got to me, I think, wasn't so much the idea that Jesus could be Jewish. It was that I already felt so attached to Jesus, I didn't want him to change. It was strange how fast this expectation of Jesus came on. I loved Jesus from the minute I saw him portrayed on the stage. My devotion to him was instantaneous and complete. I was willing to give my whole life to Jesus and had already begun to make the sacrifices I knew would have to come with my changed life. Only a few of my friends were Christians, and I knew that those who weren't would treat me the way we'd all treated Steve after he became a Christian. My family sure wasn't going to join in on this thing, and I didn't really feel like asking them to. I even sensed that I was becoming a different person in ways that were pretty destabilizing. At sixteen years old, I had no experience with the kind of loss I knew was coming, and it was almost too much for me to take. But I had Jesus and needed to believe he would be enough.

One of the first Christian albums I bought was Keith Green's *No Compromise,* and I played that cassette over and over. I remember being in my 1972 Toyota Corona listening to a song called "To Obey Is Better Than Sacrifice." I was crying so hard, I had to pull over to the side of the road. I leaned my head against the steering wheel and prayed, "Jesus, even if I never have another friend in my life, I will always live with you." I felt like I had a new best friend, a brother, a literal soul mate.

Somewhere in that first summer of my faith, I got my hands on a framed picture of Jesus (I think of it as the "vintage 1983" Jesus). It was a great picture. His hair was sandy brown and slightly windblown. He had a smile on his face and a twinkle in his eye. He looked like a guy I wanted to hang around with, a guy who was smart and funny and cool and tough and kind. He looked contemporary, like he could show up at my school and everyone would want to meet him.

This image was a big improvement over the other pictures of Jesus I'd seen around. The Christian bookstore had the Italian Jesus, with his long face and hair parted down the middle. He wasn't that bad, but he didn't look very inviting.

Still, Italian Jesus was better than Somber Jesus, the one in the weird robes with the cross on his shoulder. But even Somber Jesus was a step up from Holy Jesus with the circle around his head. I mean, this guy looked like a cartoon. How could I relate to a cartoon?

Clearly, windblown Jesus was the winner. He was tan. He was handsome. He had hope in his face. And he looked like, well, he looked like me. At least to me he did. This picture fit the image in my head—the image of Jesus who was like me and who liked me.

When that girl told me Jesus was a Jew, it was like being told he didn't get along with people or that he didn't have belly button. It just seemed so bizarre and improbable. How could I have missed something like that about my new best friend? I felt like I'd been duped. I didn't want a different Jesus, a Jewish Jesus. I liked the one I had!

I know what it's like when someone starts messing around with Jesus. I know that rethinking the nature of God, the state of humanity, the essence of sin, leads to rethinking Jesus. And I know how difficult that can be. Over the past few years, as my faith has been rearranged by my understanding of an integrated God and all the good that follows from that belief, there has been a shadowy side, a question I've hardly dared ask: What happens to Jesus?

The Greek version of the Christian story provides an ideal place for Jesus: He is the one who connects us with God. He is the bridge. He is our way out of our depraved state. He is the blood sacrifice paid out for our redemption to appease the blood God. But if there is no cosmic court case, why do we need Jesus? If there is no gap, why do we need Jesus? If sin is really our "dis-integration" with the life of God and not an ontological problem of our humanity, why do we need Jesus?

There have been times when I've talked with people about this integrated way of faith while secretly hoping they won't do the Jesus math while I'm still in the room. But inevitably, someone corners me in a hallway at church or the back of a conference room and says, "So in this 'new' way of seeing God, what becomes of Jesus? Is he just some moral teacher?" Or "So basically, you don't believe in sin anymore, and Jesus was some failed revolutionary?" Or "So you're suggesting that all religions are the same and that Christianity happens to have the Jesus logo on it even though it doesn't mean anything?" I used to dread these questions, not because I didn't want to answer them but because for quite some time I couldn't. And that scared the bejesus out of me.

I didn't know the answer to the Jesus question, but I knew this: I didn't want to follow any faith that didn't have a prime place for Jesus. But decades after that conversation in the school stairwell, I began to realize something. The Jewish connection wasn't a secret that had been kept from me. It was central to everything I'd ever understood about faith. The Hebrew story of an integrated God bringing healing and wholeness to all of creation has

I didn't know the answer to the Jesus question, but I knew this: I didn't want to follow any faith that didn't have a prime place for Jesus.

Jesus right at the center of it—the whole Bible *is* the Jesus story. The Jewish story proved to be the salvation of my Jesus.

Even as the Greek version of Christianity has taken over and we have lost the subtle beauty of the Hebrew version, that version has remained at the core of the Bible and the life of Jesus. Any Jew reading the New Testament would find a replay of Jewish history. Jesus is born in a totally impossible situation to a young mother, reminiscent of Abraham and Sarah giving birth to Isaac in their old age. Jesus survives a childhood slaughter and is sent off to Egypt, just like Moses. Jesus faces temptation in the wilderness, just like the nation of Israel. Jesus goes to a mountaintop and speaks for God, just like Moses. Jesus is the good shepherd, like David. Jesus takes on the priests like the prophets did. Jesus heals and raises the dead in the way of Elisha and Elijah. The story of Jesus is a Jewish story in all its fullness.

But to truly understand what makes Jesus essential to Christianity, I had to move beyond just knowing what Jesus did. I had to know who he was. And as usual, I discovered that the Greek worldview had covered over some rather elemental aspects of the Hebrew story, starting with the names we have for Jesus.

The name Jesus holds tremendous power in our culture. It's set apart, it's holy, it's the name above all names. Come on—anyone who isn't from a Hispanic culture has to admit to being taken aback whenever they meet someone named Jesus. When our friends the Smiths were about to have their first baby, I suggested they ought to consider calling the baby Jesus if it was a boy. We laughed at the notion of Jesus Smith—it simply doesn't fit. It's a perfectly nice name, but it just can't be used on a mere mortal.

However, there is something totally normal about the name in the first-century Jewish context. The Hebrew version of Jesus is Jeshua (the Jews would pronounce it "Joshua"). So to tell the stories of the Bible in their original context would mean using Joshua for Jesus. In fact, the telling of the Christmas story includes the famous scene of an angel coming to Joseph in a dream, telling him to marry Mary and to name the baby Joshua.[1]

That name would have made all the sense in the world to Joseph. Like all Jews, Joseph knew the story of Joshua from childhood. But few Christians today think of Joshua of the Old Testament connected with Jesus of the New. We tend to know not much more about Joshua than what we get from the Sunday school story of his army marching around the city of Jericho and blowing trumpets until the walls collapsed. But for the Jews, Joshua was supremely important. He was the one who completed the work of Moses.

The connection of Joshua to Moses was crucial in the Hebrew faith. Moses was called to lead the nation of Israel out of Egypt, putting an end to four hundred years of bondage, and into the land that God promised to Abraham's descendants. This was and is the ultimate framing story in the Jewish faith—the deliverance of the nation from bondage, the Passover, the parting of the sea, the provision in the wilderness, the giving of the ten covenant commandments.

But Moses, despite his crucial role as the faith leader, was not allowed to accompany his people into the promised land. He was not the one to bring the ultimate completion. That became the role of Joshua. He was the one who ushered in the fulfillment of God's promise.

The Jews, then, would have understood that when Jesus was referred to as Joshua, he was the one who came to finish what Moses had started. Imagine the thrill for the Jews in hearing Jesus say, "I have not come to abolish the Law of Moses, but to fulfill it."[2] In Jesus, the first-century Jews saw the completion of the story that began with Abraham, Moses, and Joshua. They saw Jesus as God's promise fulfilled. Jesus was not just a Jew; he was the promised one in the way of Joshua.

That fulfillment was the essence of Jesus. The Jews understood sin as anything that derailed them from life with God and kept them in slavery. They recognized sin as a kind of bondage, a captivity from which they needed rescue. So in the same way that Moses delivered the Israelites from Egypt and Joshua brought them into the promised land, so did this savior, Jesus, lead them into a new freedom from sin. Jesus was what was expected and hoped for. He was the promised one, the one who would bring healing and hope to all held hostage to sin.

Who knew there was so much in a name?

But the name Jesus doesn't stand alone. There are many who think, as I did for quite some time in the early days of my faith, that Jesus has a last name: Christ. (Seriously, his last name would have been something like Bar-Joseph, or Joseph's Son—in the land my ancestors come from, we would say Josephson.) The Hebrew version of the word *Christ* is *Messiah*—the same word in two different languages. But no one says "Jesus Messiah" these days, primarily because Christ is—say it with me now—the Greek word, and over time it simply became the most common way to talk about Jesus. This is likely a proper cultural adaptation of the word, but there is something much more significant that happens when Jesus has a Greek last name.

The Greek word *Christos* means "the anointed one." It is the Greek form of the word *Messiah,* which tends to stress "the promised one" as the primary meaning. It's a perfectly viable translation of the word. Yet anytime a word is translated from one language to another, some meaning is lost and other meaning is added. I don't believe for a minute that *Christ* and *Messiah* are mutually exclusive terms and that one has to give way to the other. But I think that over the centuries, as Christ has become the preeminent last name for Jesus, we've lost a significant nuance of the role of Jesus as the Messiah, the promised one.

Let me explain what I mean. Every promise has three parts: there's the one doing the promising, the one being given the promise, and the promise itself. The three hang in a delicate tension until the promise is fulfilled. And that tension is the thread that ties the Bible together.

The Hebrew faith was all about the promise—God's covenant with the nation of Israel. God's promise of rescue, of freedom, of release from bondage, is at the heart of every story in the Old Testament. It is what sustained the Jews throughout their history. So imagine what it meant to a Jew living in those earliest days of Christianity to learn that Jesus was the fulfillment of the promise given to the ancestors. Joshua Bar-Joseph wasn't just someone who was chosen or sent or anointed. Jesus the Messiah was the one who was promised, the one who was expected and hoped for and waited for for thousands of years. Jesus was God doing what God always said God would do.

This view of Jesus also brings with it a deeper sense of God's connection with humanity. The term *Messiah* has this sense of Jesus being an ambassador. It suggests that Jesus came with the authority of God to carry out the agenda of God; there's a kind of historicity about it. It's embedded in something that came before—the promise itself. Time and time again, as people struggle and rebel and break apart, God points them to the promise. God reminds them that they are never alone, never abandoned, never truly lost. This promise—and the promised one—are God's continued connection with humanity.

> Jesus the Messiah was the one who was promised, the one who was expected and hoped for and waited for for thousands of years. Jesus was God doing what God always said God would do.

There is never a gap in this connection. There is never a time when God pulls the covenant off the table. There is never a time when God rejects the people and breaks the promise. The promise of rescue is there in every moment. The Messiah, then, doesn't stand alone in a particular time and place as a special anointed one. Rather the Messiah is in this eternal relationship with God; he is ever-connected to the one who sent him.

The Gentiles, of course, didn't feel the power of the promise the way the Jews did. They were far more familiar with the Greco-Roman version of the gods. So the Messiah image didn't carry the same weight for the Gentiles as it did for the Jews. Remember that the Greeks and Romans had a pantheon of gods who were pretentious and hard to please. These gods toyed with the emotions and lives of humans for the fun of it. When humans displeased the gods, the gods would invoke punishment in order to force repentance. So as Christianity spread, the early evangelists recognized that they could help the Jesus story make sense if Jesus was seen as someone who was chosen to appease the wrath of God—hence, the "anointed one" who could do what no one else could do. And this rang true to the Gentiles.

This wasn't just a name issue. Jesus was the Savior for both the Jews and the Gentiles. But the two groups had vastly different ideas about what it was Jesus was saving them from. The Gentiles thought of Jesus as saving them from the punishment that was due them. Jesus became the substitute, the stand-in. He was the special, divine, innocent one chosen by God to pay the price for the sins of humanity. That's what the up-and-out, distant, vengeful God demanded.

But the Jewish God was a loving father figure, the down-and-in God who provided for the people and called them to join in with God's work in the world. This God was an intimate lover who pursued his beloved people with all that was necessary to bring them fully into life with him. So the Messiah was their map, their guide to what true partnership with God looked like. They weren't left to wander on their own. They had the living, breathing promise of God to show them the way. The Messiah restored them to the lives for which they were created. This common man with a common name was God saying, "I love you still and want you, whoever you are, to come with me."

Jesus was living in the midst of a history, the history of Israel. To know Jesus is to know him as a Jew calling us to join with the ancient story of God calling Abraham and his descendants to be a blessing to all the world. It is to follow Jesus as Joshua into the promised land of freedom and release. It is to believe that Jesus is not only the Christ but the one who came to fulfill the agenda of God. He is the Prince of Peace, the Word made Flesh, the Savior and Lord, the King of Kings, the Lion of Judah, the Lamb of God, the Son of God, the Son of Man. This is Jesus the Jew, the Messiah of God.

"Jesus was a Jew, you know?"

Now that is truly good news.

16

YOU SAY YOU WANT A REVOLUTION

In my early years of Christian faith, a few of us would spend our weekends and summer nights hanging out in Minneapolis with homeless people, prostitutes, and downtrodden kids. I was just out of high school myself, and having come from an "accept people for who they are" kind of family, I felt pretty comfortable being with other young people who were trying to find their way on their own, no matter how rough their lives were.

My Christian friends and I didn't know much about evangelism, but we knew that God was alive in the world and wanted people to be healed and whole. So we would talk to prostitutes about other options for getting the money they needed to survive. We would buy dinner for homeless men and hang out with lonely kids. We didn't hand out tracts or invite them to our church (since we didn't have one), but we did talk to them about God and how Jesus was changing our lives. We tried to do our best to do what Jesus might have done.

We had hooked in with a group of young skate punks at one of the lakes in the city. We'd show up on Friday nights and watch them skate, tell them stories about God, and talk about life. We were sincere, and so were they. Now these kids were among the first wave of skater kids in Minnesota. Long before skateboarding came with sponsorships and X-Games on ESPN, it was an antisocial activity of deviant kids. There were four guys in the group we knew from the lake. They wore eyeliner, smoked, dressed in anarchy T-shirts, and spat on the sidewalks. They knew the rules against skateboarding on the dock at Lake Harriet and were masters at avoiding the bike police.

One Friday night Steve—the friend who brought me to the Passion Play—Shelley, and I arrived at the lake to find a crowd of people gathered around the dock. Even from a distance, we could hear them cheering and jeering. As we looked through the crowd toward the lake, we could see one of our skater friends pulling himself out of the water and onto the dock. It was clear from the reaction of the crowd that this kid had just been thrown into the lake. Two much bigger guys were standing near him, laughing.

I asked someone in the crowd what was happening. He explained that the group was football players and cheerleaders from Armstrong, a large suburban high school, who were on a group outing to the lake. There had been some altercation with our young friend, and these football players were bringing the consequences.

We looked back toward the dock. Our guy was standing there, spitting mad and gearing up to regain his pride. There was no doubt he was going to get beaten up—the guys who threw him in the lake had as much pride to keep as the skater had just lost. Just as the kid was dragging his wet body and board toward the football players, I noticed that Steve had slipped through the crowd and toward our friend. Steve was five-foot-ten and 195 pounds and was wearing his ever-present overly large yellow backpack—quite an intimidating sight in his own way. As the skater moved toward his hulking enemies, Steve stepped in front of him, turned to the two mountains of muscle, and yelled, "Hey, if you want to throw someone in the lake, you can throw me."

I had no idea what was going on. Steve continued, "That's right. I can handle rejection. My mom left my family my first day of kindergarten. My dad has a drug addiction and abused me and my friends. I've been kicked out of school, lived for years in a foster home, and beat my own drug habit. I can handle the rejection."

Then, in one seamless move, Steve reached over his shoulder like a Samurai warrior and pulled his huge Bible out of his backpack. He shouted, "I'll tell you someone else who was rejected: Jesus."

With that he started preaching. It was surreal. And it was perfect. The image of Steve likening our punk friend to the beaten and rejected Jesus and then standing alongside him as a fellow reject was priceless.

The crowd slowly dispersed, and even the skater kids decided not to stick around—there is only so much of a "crazy" street preacher anyone can handle. We didn't see much of them after that night, and who knows if Steve's decision to stand up for the beaten down made any difference to them. But I know it made a difference to me. I saw it so clearly: The story of Jesus as good news for a kid who didn't get beaten up. I saw it as good news for everyone who is put down and abandoned and left behind. God is ever with you.

Steve didn't know it (and neither did I), but as he stood on the end of the dock that night, he was preaching the gospel according to the Jews. The Greek gospel is about the distant God coming into contact with lowly humanity through the atoning life, death, and resurrection of Jesus the Christ, the perfect, sinless Son of God. And

Jesus the Messiah stood alongside the oppressed and imprisoned, the rejected and the lost, as a sign of God's connection and closeness.

there is certainly an appeal in that kind in view. But for the Jews, Jesus was the lowly one. Jesus the Messiah stood alongside the oppressed and imprisoned, the rejected and the lost, as a sign of God's connection and closeness. Jesus was their promised rescuer. Jesus was good news for the Jews even before he died and was resurrected.

This is where the "what happened to Jesus" question gets a little more meaty for me. As I learned more about the Jewish Jesus, I felt both an incredible sense of relief and a rather disconcerting fear. I had a much better sense of who Jesus was and the importance of his Jewish heritage. But there were questions that continued to nag me. Things like, if the first-century Jews understood Jesus as the Messiah, why aren't Jews Christians today? And if the arrival of Jesus was the intended fulfillment of God's promise to the nation of Israel, what was the point of Jesus' death and resurrection? Wasn't his life enough?

The answers to these questions involve some rather heady history and theology that I'm still trying to sort out. But here's the best understanding I have of why Jesus still belongs at the center of my understanding of Christianity as partnering with God.

The story of Jesus unfolds in the midst of personal and collective struggle. This will take a bit of context to make sense. So at the risk of sounding like a Hebrew school teacher, let me paint a brief picture. The story of Jesus is surrounded by the death of individuals and communities, by the constant stirring of war. For the Jews in particular, the first century was a volatile, violent time. The Jews were literally fighting to save their culture and their faith. The preceding three hundred years had been full of small military victories, but as a whole, the Jews' situation had changed greatly from the time of Abraham. It was in God's promise to Abraham[1] that the Jews found their sense of calling and purpose—to be a blessing to all the world. But the Jews continued to be an oppressed people. Time and time again, they were displaced, enslaved, despised. The Old Testament rumbles with the cry of the Jewish people: "How long, oh Lord?" Their desperation is palpable.

That desperation created conflict between the Jews, the occupying Romans, and other religious and ethnic groups, but it also created conflict within the Jewish faith itself. The Jews were not monolithically single-minded. The Jewish faith changed in response to culture and history, just like the Christian faith has done. That's why we see Jesus interacting with various groups of Jewish people throughout the four Gospels. There were the Pharisees, the Teachers of the Law, the Sadducees, the commoners, and the reputed sinners. There were the zealots—a religious group that stirred up a military revolution. (It may well have been this group that finally raged against Rome in A.D. 70, to which the Romans responded by destroying the Temple, which has never been rebuilt.) There were the Essenes (John the Baptist may have been associated with this group), who believed that the Jews ought to separate themselves from a shared life with the pagans and instead live on their own in the wilderness as the nation of Israel. Some Jews were deeply embedded in Greek customs, while others sought to maintain cultural purity. Some kept away from all things Roman, and some cooperated readily with the occupying nation.

And there were differing ideas on the future of the world. Some Jews held to a destructive, apocalyptic view. They believed that one day God would make all things right by bringing justice and healing to the world, that in doing so God would bring a giant, cosmic smackdown on all who were in opposition to God—namely, the godless Gentiles. Another group of Jews never held to a messianic age of any kind. There were Jews who didn't believe in an afterlife or in a resurrection and others who built their orientation fully on a resurrection.

Jesus, then, lived in a time of significant political, religious, and structural turmoil. War was on everyone's mind. The Romans used great force to keep the Jews from revolting against the Romans' brutal repression. Some Jews wanted to take up arms against the Romans and did so on many occasions.

This war impulse is played out in the story of Jesus' arrest, right before his crucifixion, which itself was primarily the result of Rome seeking to prevent a revolt. In an attempt to keep Jesus from being abducted, the disciple Peter strikes a guard on the side of the head, cutting off his ear. This is a brutal scene. The blood flows, and tempers flare. Clearly, Peter was willing to kill to protect Jesus.

I'd always understood this story as Peter sticking up for his friend, but now I think there's much more to it than that. This wasn't one man defending another. This was a man defending a revolutionary cause. Peter didn't hesitate to jump into battle because he believed that was why Jesus had come—to lead the Jews to victory over the Romans. In Peter's mind this was it, the moment they'd been waiting for. This was to be the turning point in Jewish history. (The strength of Peter's conviction is significant, not only in this story but in the book of Acts, where Peter comes to believe that the gospel is intended for the Greeks as well as the Jews. His dramatic shift in understanding literally took an act of God.)[2]

Reading the arrest story with the backdrop of revolution in mind makes Jesus' response even more interesting. He says, "Put your sword back in its place, for all who draw the sword will die by the sword."[3]

Many of the Jews were primed for a revolution, with their swords at the ready. And as Jesus was proclaimed the Messiah, the expectation of that big smackdown bubbled up around him. There were those, like Peter, who were just waiting for the moment when Jesus would unleash the full power of heaven to destroy the Romans and free the Jews once and for all.

This notion, commonly conjured up in the phrase "the day of the Lord," was one of the first tenets of certain sects of Jewish theology to get upended by first-century Christianity. Instead, Christianity proclaimed that Jesus was the Messiah who would right the world by ushering in the reign of love and partnership, not by demolishing the enemies of God. The idea that evil and oppression could remain after the so-called deliverance of the people is one of the major reasons many Jews reject the idea of Jesus as the Messiah. How could the Messiah have come and the apocalyptic agenda not be fulfilled?

It wasn't only Jesus' position as the Messiah that gave the Jews the expectation he would lead them to war. His very name fit with his calling to be a warrior; Joshua was a warrior as well. Joshua Messiah—the warrior, the promised one. You can hardly blame the Jews for feeling like they were in the middle of a little bait-and-switch here.

But Jesus was about a different kind of revolution. He was about a revolution from the kingdom of Caesar to the kingdom of God. In our day, that language of kingdoms has an antique, Camelot feel to it—knights and kings and castles. But in Jesus' day the kingdom of God, or kingdom of heaven, sat in contrast to the kingdom of the Roman rule of Caesar. In many ways it also sat in contrast to the kingdom-of-David agenda hailed by many of the Jews. (Some Jews had the idea that if they could get back to the "glory days," as when David was the king of Israel, all would be well.) But for Jesus there was an even better end, one where all people, not just the Jews, were central players in the kingdom of God.

Some theologians have dissected all of this by talking about spiritual kingdoms and wars verses earthly kingdoms and wars. They argue that Jesus did bring about a kind of war in which the power of good battles the power of evil and that Christians are to be warriors who fight against the darkness that oppresses us, knowing that one day Jesus will ride out of the sky and defeat the enemy at last. I suppose that's one way of thinking about all of this, but I think there's more to Jesus than a change of metaphor.

It seems to me that the way of Jesus is not just to shift the war motif from one kind of war to another but to see Jesus as the ender of war, period. Jesus brought with him the hope that the people would no longer see themselves in the midst of a war but would join with God in the healing of all the world.

> It seems to me that the way of Jesus is not just to shift the war motif from one kind of war to another but to see Jesus as the ender of war, period.

Holding this view of Jesus involves seeing the ways in which his life is in line with the messianic mission laid out in the vision of the prophet Isaiah. In the Gospel of Luke, we read about Jesus going to great lengths to connect his life to the words of Isaiah. At the start of his public efforts, Jesus entered the synagogue and announced his mission. He declared that the kingdom of God, not the kingdom of Caesar or David, was near and that all were invited to live in it. Here's how Luke tells the story:

> [Jesus] went to Nazareth, where he had been brought up, and on the Sabbath day he went into the synagogue, as was his custom. He stood up to read, and the scroll of the prophet Isaiah was handed to him. Unrolling it, he found the place where it is written:
>
> "The Spirit of the Lord is on me, because he has anointed me to proclaim good news to the poor. He has sent me to proclaim freedom for the prisoners and recovery of sight for the blind, to set the oppressed free, to proclaim the year of the Lord's favor."
>
> Then he rolled up the scroll, gave it back to the attendant and sat down. The eyes of everyone in the synagogue were fastened on him. He began by saying to them, "Today this scripture is fulfilled in your hearing."[4]

Jesus was not only the new Joshua coming to lead the people toward all that God had promised; he was the new Isaiah who had come to usher in that promise in a particular way. This wasn't metaphorical language. Jesus wasn't bringing some kind of future-based spiritual good news to the poor. He was inviting them into life with God in the present. The release of prisoners Jesus spoke of had real-life connotations, and every imprisoned Jew knew it. So did the Roman rulers. Jesus healed literal blindness, not just spiritual blindness. His proclamation of the year of the Lord's favor conjured up all the hopes of those who wanted the apocalyptic retribution to come, but the Lord's favor came not through war but through a holy act that conquered death forever.

I have come to believe in Jesus as the Messiah who came to bring these words of Isaiah to life:

> Nevertheless, there will be no more gloom for those who were in distress. In the past he humbled the land of Zebulun and the land of Naphtali, but in the future he will honor Galilee of the nations, by the Way of the Sea, beyond the Jordan—
>
> The people walking in darkness have seen a great light; on those living in the land of deep darkness a light has dawned. You have enlarged the nation and increased their joy; they rejoice before you as people rejoice at the harvest, as soldiers rejoice when dividing the plunder.
>
> For as in the day of Midian's defeat, you have shattered the yoke that burdens them, the bar across their shoulders, the rod of their oppressor. Every warrior's boot used in battle and every garment rolled in blood will be destined for burning, will be fuel for the fire.
>
> For to us a child is born, to us a son is given, and the government will be on his shoulders. And he will be called Wonderful Counselor, Mighty God, Everlasting Father, Prince of Peace.
>
> Of the increase of his government and peace there will be no end. He will reign on David's throne and over his

kingdom, establishing and upholding it with justice and righteousness from that time on and forever. The zeal of the LORD Almighty will accomplish this.[5]

It seems to me that this is what rescue ought to look like. It doesn't look like more war; it looks like the end of war. The very elements of battle—the boots and blood-stained clothes—become a source of life, of hope.

Jesus was not sent as the selected one to appease the anger of the Greek blood god. Jesus was sent to fulfill the promise of the Hebrew love God by ending human hostility. It was not the anger of God that Jesus came to end but the anger of people. This world God created is one of peace and harmony and integration. Through Jesus, all humanity is brought into that world. And that is the point of the resurrection.

The story of Jesus Christ, of Joshua the Messiah, is about the healing all of creation. This was God's promise from the start—that people would be God's partners in the world. When Jesus was resurrected from the dead, life won out. The power of God's love for humanity proved stronger than our capacity to hate one another. Jesus' death was about war, about violence, about destruction. But his resurrection was about peace, compassion, renewal. The resurrection is the full picture of God's promise.

> **Jesus was sent to fulfill the promise of the Hebrew love God by ending human hostility. It was not the anger of God that Jesus came to end but the anger of people.**

The Christian faith finds its center in the story of Jesus not because this is where the problem of God's anger is solved. Jesus is the core of Christianity because it is through Jesus that we see the fullness of God's hopes for the world. Jesus is the redemption of the creation plan. He shows us what it means to live in partnership with our creator. He leads us into what it means to be integrated with God.

Resurrection is not a do-over. We don't move on as though nothing ever happened. No, redeemed life is a new kind of life. Jesus was resurrected with scars. The scars weren't simply a reminder of the past; they were the pathway to the future. They were there to show that the cause of death had been consumed. The hatred of death had been healed over by the love of God. The resurrection wasn't like a last-minute save by the divine goalkeeper. The scars gave testimony to the power of death. Death gave Jesus its best shot; it laid it all on the line and accomplished it goal. But life overcame death. Love overcame hate. Peace overcame war. The resurrection life needs death to remind us that the call to love our enemy not only means loving in the midst of scars but loving those who cause them. Because in Jesus, love wins.

17

I DIDN'T KNOW HIM FROM ADAM

I attended my first—and only—Christian protest in 1984. I have never been much of a protester, but I was new to faith and willing to do just about anything to help spread the fabulous news of God's invitation. So when some friends suggested we go stand up for our faith, I was all for it.

We headed over to the Cooper Theater in Saint Louis Park, where we planned to use our signs and words to convince people that they should stay away from the movie *The Last Temptation of Christ*. But our plan had a fatal flaw: none of us had seen the movie. So when we told people they shouldn't see the movie and they asked why not, we didn't have a very good answer. I remember one woman in particular. She realized we were protesting a movie we hadn't seen, and she was completely confused. I had gone into this protest with some kind of conviction, but it was starting to waver. So I offered a totally lame explanation that went something like this: "Well, you don't need to taste dirt to know you don't like it, do you?"

I knew it was a pathetic response, but I said it with all the confidence I could muster. The truth was, I really wanted to know what this movie was about. All I had to go on was that Christians of all stripes were warning people against the blasphemy it contained. The pope, my friends, preachers on TV—all of them were telling viewers to stay away. From what I'd heard, the movie was heresy because it raised questions about the divinity of Jesus, questions that these voices of the church felt were way out of bounds. And if that was the case, it was my duty as a Christian to stand up for Jesus and prevent people from seeing that movie.

When I finally saw the movie years later, my first thought was that it was a good thing I hadn't seen it when I was seventeen. I would have been bored out of my mind (it's one of those slow, artsy films). But I also would have been totally confused. At seventeen, I certainly hadn't given any thought to the central premise of the movie: How could Jesus be fully God and fully human at the same time? And if Jesus was human, how human was he? Did he struggle like a normal person? Did he want to die on the cross? I would have missed the significance of these questions, even though the pope and every other Christian I knew seemed to think they were deal breakers. Honestly, I would have wondered what the big problem was.

The movie deals with these questions through a series of visions Jesus has while hanging on the cross, visions of coming off the cross and living a "normal" life. He ultimately resists this "temptation," choosing instead to remain on the cross. The movie doesn't suggest some alternative ending to the Jesus story, but the mere suggestion of these human questions raised the hackles of many people in the church.

The questions of this movie were part of a long debate among the learned faithful. Years before *The Da Vinci Code* popularized the theory, that idea that Jesus was just a normal guy who led a campaign of moral virtue, married Mary Magdalene, and raised a family, a guy who had his message stolen and turned into a religion by guys like the apostle Paul, was well known to biblical scholars and church leaders. But when this movie suggested a version of that story line to the general public, the reaction was swift and sure.

Thinking back on the furor over *The Last Temptation of Christ*, I'm struck not only by my willingness to take a stand against something I really didn't know anything about but also by the depth and strength of the church's reaction to the movie. It's not that I think the questions the movie explored are unimportant. It's that they have always been woven into the Jesus story. They are as essential to understanding Jesus as knowing his name. They have never been secret, never been out of bounds. They are all over the New Testament.

This mix of the human and the divine was a puzzle even before Jesus was born. Mary, the mother of Jesus, wondered what kind of child she was carrying.[1] At Jesus' circumcision, Simeon spoke of the power shift that would come through this child.[2] The disciples were awed when Jesus calmed a storm.[3] All the way through the history of the church, there have been attempts to make sense of the nature of Jesus.

This isn't an issue reserved for apostles, theologians, or filmmakers. It sits at the heart of disagreements between Muslims and Christians, Christians and Jews, Protestants and Catholics. It is an issue of tremendous significance for every ordinary person who wants to understand what it means to know Jesus.

As you might imagine, I am going to suggest that this question—and the answers we've been given—has been significantly influenced by the Greek version of Christianity. And it has. The very structure of the question and what too often passes for a viable answer are inextricably connected to Christianity's Greek history.

To the Greek mind, the idea that humanity and divinity could interact, let alone coexist in one body, was unthinkable. The Hebrew mind, on the other hand, found this much more acceptable. So a Jew could say, as the apostle Paul did, that "God was pleased to have all his fullness dwell in [Jesus]."[4] But a few centuries into the faith, this kind of statement only raised new questions that needed to be answered. And answer the church did.

This human-divine issue was so confounding for the church that it made various attempts at developing an "official" statement concerning the nature of Jesus. In the fourth century, the Council of Nicaea took a stab at an explanation:

> One Lord Jesus Christ, the only-begotten Son of God, begotten of the Father before all worlds, God of God, Light of Light, Very God of Very God, begotten, not made, being of one substance with the Father by whom all things were made;
>
> Who for us men, and for our salvation, came down from heaven, and was incarnate by the Holy Spirit of the Virgin Mary, and was made man.[5]

The Westminster Confession of Faith, written in the seventeenth century, goes to even greater lengths to sort this out, stating:

> The Son of God, the second person of the Trinity, being very and eternal God, of one substance and equal with the Father, did, when the fullness of time was come, take upon Him man's nature, with all the essential properties, and common infirmities thereof, yet without sin; being conceived by the power of the Holy Ghost, in the womb of the virgin Mary, of her substance. So that two whole, perfect, and distinct natures, the Godhead and the manhood, were inseparably joined together in one person,

without conversion, composition, or confusion. Which person is very God, and very man, yet one Christ, the only Mediator between God and man.[6]

The Council of Chalcedon created a creed that is exclusively intended to clear up any confusion about Jesus. It says:

> Therefore, following the holy fathers, we all with one accord teach men to acknowledge one and the same Son, our Lord Jesus Christ, at once complete in Godhead and complete in manhood, truly God and truly man, consisting also of a reasonable soul and body; of one substance with the Father as regards his Godhead, and at the same time of one substance with us as regards his manhood; like us in all respects, apart from sin; as regards his Godhead, begotten of the Father before the ages, but yet as regards his manhood begotten, for us men and for our salvation, of Mary the Virgin, the God-bearer; one and the same Christ, Son, Lord, Only-begotten, recognized in two natures, without confusion, without change, without division, without separation; the distinction of natures being in no way annulled by the union, but rather the characteristics of each nature being preserved and coming together to form one person and subsistence, not as parted or separated into two persons, but one and the same Son and Only-begotten God the Word, Lord Jesus Christ; even as the prophets from earliest times spoke of him, and our Lord Jesus Christ himself taught us, and the creed of the fathers has handed down to us.[7]

There's no question that these statements have been helpful and important in the life of the church, but they can only go so far. They can't remove the conflict embedded in the worldview that keeps divinity and humanity at odds. And they can't help but perpetuate the notion that Jesus was some sort of strange breed of being—part God and part human, some kind of superhero who lived a life no one else could possibly live. If we hold to a Jesus made of "God fabric," something wholly unlike the fabric that makes up the rest of humanity, then what hope do we have of living godly lives? Living faithfully in the way of Jesus becomes an impossible— and cruel—expectation. It makes these words of Jesus sound like a joke: "Very truly I tell you, all who have faith in me will do the works I have been doing, and they will do even greater things than these, because I am going to the Father."[8]

A Catholic friend of mine once told me that many Catholic girls struggle with their self-esteem because they are told to live like the Virgin Mary. She said, "It's a little tough to live up to the expectation that we are to be both a virgin and a mother." It's difficult to live a life of faithfulness when the pattern was set by someone so "other."

Greco-Roman mythology contributed to this worldview in which divine interaction in the human world led to heroic figures like Hercules and Perseus. For the Greeks, anyone who was part god and part human was no ordinary human. And just as no ordinary Greek would have assumed that he could live like Hercules (the Greeks called him Heracles), no ordinary Greek Christian would have assumed he could live like Jesus.

It's this mash-up of Greek myth and the Jesus story that led some theologians in the early centuries to suggest that Jesus was not human at all but an energy force who didn't eat food or leave footprints when he walked. The theory implied that Jesus never actually touched people but emanated a force that healed them. This might sound crazy to us, but within the context of that Greek worldview, where the divine was the opposite of the human, this superhuman Christ made sense.

These kinds of concerns don't show up in the New Testament because New Testament Christianity was mainly explained through a Hebrew lens. The Jews understood Jesus as the Messiah, a title that wasn't riddled with superhero connotations. The Messiah was part of the family, as it were. Jesus the Messiah wasn't an anomaly in the Hebrew story; he was the next chapter. The Jews always believed that their Messiah would rise up from within their community, that he would be one of them. And that's who Jesus was: the Messiah, born the poor son of a

The Jews always believed that their Messiah would rise up from within their community, that he would be one of them. And that's who Jesus was.

Jewish carpenter, who walked alongside his friends, his family, his people.

The Gospel of Luke lays out Jesus' family tree, tracing his lineage all the way back through Jewish history—from David to Abraham to Noah to Adam. Jesus was part of the plan from the beginning, and the entire story of the Hebrew people leads right to him. Every Jew knew that the prophetic words of Isaiah and Jeremiah pointed to a savior who was one of them. So they understood Jesus as the new Joshua and the new David. But the Jews also knew that Jesus was more that that. They knew that Jesus was the new Adam.

The belief in Jesus as the new Adam speaks directly to this issue of the humanity of Jesus. Again, the mysterious mix of the human and the divine wasn't the same kind of problem for the Jewish followers of Jesus as it was for the Greeks. Their worldview allowed for a God who was integrated with humanity; actually, their view of the world *depended* on it.

The story of the covenant between God and Israel was one the Jews traced back to Moses. In their view, the Law was put into place when Moses received the Ten Commandments. Since the Law applied only to the Jews, it made sense to them that the promise inherent in the Law applied only to them as well. The tumultuous history that followed confirmed the belief that the Jews were set apart for a special relationship with God.

Once Jesus arrived on the scene, the Jews believed that this astonishing fulfillment of God's promise was just for them. And that made sense: they were the ones who'd been living in captivity. It was their history that was riddled with slavery and oppression and displacement. They had suffered and survived because of their faith in the covenant between themselves and their God. From their perspective, there was no way God intended to offer freedom and partnership to the Greeks, the very people who had oppressed and enslaved and displaced them. No, the Greeks, the Romans, the non-Jews of every stripe were the enemy, and they were to be put in their proper place by the new Joshua. They were to be ruled over by the new David.

But within a few years of the resurrection, there were Greek Christians, which caused no end of consternation for the Jewish Christians. (The book of Acts and much of the book of Romans revolve around this ongoing controversy and its implications.) It was the apostle Paul (who had been a Jew who persecuted Christians for "perverting" the Jewish faith until he literally saw the light and came to Jesus) who explained to the church in Rome, a Gentile population center, why the gospel and the promise fulfilled in Jesus was for all people, not just the Jews.

Paul explained that the promise of Moses was for the Jews but that God also included the Gentiles by going back not only to the Moses story but to the story of Abraham; the Gentiles were included through the faith of Abraham. Then Paul went one step further and said that Jesus is not just a new Moses for the Jews, not just a new Abraham for all people, but a new Adam for all of creation. With this understanding of Jesus, Paul fully extended the Jesus story all the way back to the beginning so that he could push the story forward, opening it up to include the whole earth and everything in it.

In Romans, Paul suggests that what Adam did in his disobedience and sin affected all of creation. What Jesus as the "second Adam" did through his resurrection was heal and reconcile all of creation. It's helpful to read Paul's letter to the followers of Jesus living in Rome because it is packed with this very complex clarification of what it was that Jesus came to accomplish. I'm tempted to include the whole fourth chapter of Romans, but for the sake of space I've included only sections—it's much better to read the whole chapter, or even the whole book of Romans, to get a feel for what Paul is saying. I've also added a few parenthetical explanations to help summarize Paul's thinking.

> It was not through the law *(of Moses)* that Abraham and his offspring received the promise that he would be heir of the world, but through the righteousness that comes

by faith. *(Abraham didn't have the law of Moses, so he didn't need it to be part of God's promise and plan.)* For if those who depend on the law are heirs, faith means nothing and the promise is worthless, because the law brings wrath. And where there is no law there is no transgression. Therefore, the promise comes by faith, so that it may be by grace and may be guaranteed to all Abraham's offspring—not only to those who are of the law but also to those who have the faith of Abraham. He is the father of us all. As it is written: "I have made you a father of many nations." He is our father in the sight of God, in whom he believed—the God who gives life to the dead and calls into being things that were not. *(So all are part of the promise not because they are Jews but because they are part of the faith family of Abraham.)*

Against all hope, Abraham in hope believed and so became the father of many nations, just as it had been said to him, "So shall your offspring be." Without weakening in his faith, he faced the fact that his body was as good as dead—since he was about a hundred years old—and that Sarah's womb was also dead. Yet he did not waver through unbelief regarding the promise of God, but was strengthened in his faith and gave glory to God, being fully persuaded that God had power to do what he had promised. This is why "it was credited to him as righteousness." The words "it was credited to him" were written not for him alone, but also for us, to whom God will credit righteousness—for us who believe in him who raised Jesus our Lord from the dead. He was delivered over to death for our sins and was raised to life for our justification. *(What connects us to the faith of Abraham is the faith in God that comes as a result of the resurrection.)*

Therefore, since we have been justified through faith, we have peace with God through our Lord Jesus Christ, through whom we have gained access by faith into this grace in which we now stand. And we boast in the hope of the glory of God. *(It is through the resurrection of Jesus that the promise is extended.)*

Since we have now been justified by his blood, how much more shall we be saved from God's wrath through him! For if, while we were God's enemies, we were reconciled to him through the death of his Son, how much more, having been reconciled, shall we be saved through his life! Not only is this so, but we also boast in God through our Lord Jesus Christ, through whom we have now received reconciliation. *(Those who lived in opposition to the agenda of God are brought back into partnership with God through the resurrection. The life of Jesus points to the reconciliation of the world with God and God's agenda.)*

(Having made the point that all people are part of this story through Abraham, Paul now connects Jesus to Adam and broadens the implication for all creation.) Therefore, just as sin entered the world through one man *(Adam)*, and death through sin, and in this way death came to all people, because all sinned—to be sure, sin was in the world before the law *(of Moses)* was given, but sin is not charged against anyone's account where there is no law. Nevertheless, death reigned from the time of Adam to the time of Moses, even over those who did not sin by breaking a command *(So sin was alive as hostility and disintegration with God before there was any law or rule to be broken, and it still brought about death.)*, as did Adam, who is a pattern of the one to come. *(Here is where the idea of Jesus*

being the second Adam kicks in. Just as Adam was the pattern of disobedience, so Jesus is the new pattern of harmony.)

But the gift is not like the trespass. For if the many died by the trespass of the one man, how much more did God's grace and the gift that came by the grace of the one man, Jesus Christ, overflow to the many! *(This story of reconciliation is even better than the trespass of Adam in that it undoes the effects of sin.)*[9]

Paul's point was that even though the story of Jesus is connected to Moses, it is really a story that started with Adam. The lineage laid out in Luke's gospel makes the gospel good news for all people.

Jesus is the fulfillment of what people are meant to do, who we are meant to be. Just as Adam showed us what disobedience looks like, Jesus shows us what full integration looks like. Just as Adam made disharmony with God possible, Jesus made partnership with God attainable. He is our way, our truth, our life, our Messiah.

This kind of talk makes some Christians nervous. Some can only hear this version as a way of saying that Jesus was little more than a really great guy we should try to emulate—very nice and wishy-washy, just the opposite of the superhero

If someone were to suggest that Jesus' mission was to be a swell fellow and give us all some great tips on how to live, well, that's not the kind of faith I'm interested in.

Jesus. But if someone were to suggest that Jesus' mission was to be a swell fellow and give us all some great tips on how to live, well, that's not the kind of faith I'm interested in.

There's something special going on in the Jesus story. He isn't a superhero, and he isn't just a great example. After generations of disintegration, Jesus tells us to come with him, to follow in his way, to join in with the life of God. He tells his followers, *shows* his followers, what it looks like to live in harmony with God. Because Jesus is the Son of God, he is the very model of complete integration with the Creator. And because Jesus is the Son of Humanity, he is the very model of living out that integration in the midst of war, pain, joy, conflict, persecution, love, loss, and fear.

In the Gospel of John, Jesus himself explains who he is and what he came to show us. Jesus is trying to help his followers understand that he's going to leave them soon, and they ought to do as he had been doing. He is calling them—and us—to live as he did, to join our lives with God and God's agenda. And he assures us that it is absolutely possible.

> "Do not let your hearts be troubled. Trust in God; trust also in me. My Father's house has plenty of room; if that were not so, would I have told you that I am going there to prepare a place for you? And if I go and prepare a place for you, I will come back and take you to be with me that you also may be where I am. You know the way to the place where I am going."
>
> Thomas said to him, "Lord, we don't know where you are going, so how can we know the way?"
>
> Jesus answered, "I am the way and the truth and the life. No one comes to the Father except through me. If you

really know me, you will know my Father as well. From now on, you do know him and have seen him."

Philip said, "Lord, show us the Father and that will be enough for us."

Jesus answered: "Don't you know me, Philip, even after I have been among you such a long time? Anyone who has seen me has seen the Father. How can you say, 'Show us the Father'? Don't you believe that I am in the Father, and that the Father is in me? The words I say to you I do not speak on my own authority. Rather, it is the Father, living in me, who is doing his work. Believe me when I say that I am in the Father and the Father is in me; or at least believe on the evidence of the works themselves. Very truly I tell you, all who have faith in me will do the works I have been doing, and they will do even greater things than these, because I am going to the Father."[10]

Here in John—and throughout the gospels—we see Jesus calling his disciples to take the path he was taking, to drink the cup he was drinking, to follow God the way he followed God. He even had the audacity to hope that his followers would do even greater things than he had done. Jesus wasn't asking them to do something impossible. He wasn't asking them to give it their best shot while secretly

> We see Jesus calling his disciples to take the path he was taking, to drink the cup he was drinking, to follow God the way he followed God.

knowing they would fail. No, Jesus expected them to follow his path. He believed they could do it.

For Jews, the Torah (the first five books of the Bible) was the law of God. It was referred to as the way, truth, and life. In Psalm 119, the psalmist harks back to the law in nearly every line, for it is through the law that he knows God, follows God, praises God, and lives with God. So when Jesus uses the phrase "I am the way and the truth and the life," his listeners would have understood that he was saying he was the one through whom they would know God, follow God, praise God, and live with God. Jesus is saying that the way to God is to walk the path Jesus walked, the path of obedience, of integration, of partnership.

That's why it matters that life and love won out. The point of the resurrection was to recalibrate the balance of creation, to bring all of it into sync with the agenda of God. The resurrection was God showing us, through Jesus, that living out the agenda of God means living out an agenda of love and life.

Jesus was clear that his mission was to bring about a new kind of life, a new kind of law, a new kind of rhythm—the life, law, and rhythm of God. He invited humanity to join in with God. He was saying to his followers, "This is what life with God looks like. This is it. And you can live this life, too."

This invitation has been strikingly good news to me. It has brought hope and passion to my faith. I feel like I've been released from a faith focused on appeasing a God of unattainable expectations. Jesus' life, death, and resurrection are no longer ancient events that hold only a vague meaning for me in the afterlife. They are a road map for the life I was created to live. They are the call to that partnership for which I was made. After decades of Christianity, the Jewish understanding of Jesus as the Messiah, as the new Joshua, the new David, the new Adam, showed me that I was not called to live apart from God while I wait for death to release me from the prison of my sinful body. I was meant to live a life in full abandon. I don't need to fear God. I don't need to fear life. I don't need to fear anything. The resurrection has freed me.

18

HEAVEN ON EARTH

About a year ago a friend of mine asked me to preach at his church. This church was still in its first year, having been birthed by another church that wanted to expand its ministry to young adults. The hope was that it would be a Generation X church. So my friend had been attempting to help this start-up church consider new ways of living as a faith community.

His hope was to create a community with different values and a different focus than those of the home church. He was trying to tell the Christian story using some of the general ideas of postmodernism and emerging theology. He believed that this shift was necessary if his church was going to minister as a different group of people. He wasn't angry at or disillusioned with his previous church. He wasn't rejecting it or reacting against it. Rather, like the Celtic Christians, he was following "another bird."

His vision for the life of this new church was met with a great deal of skepticism from those who wanted him to create a duplicate of the previous church. Since his journey of hope and discovery was much like my own, he asked if I could come and talk about some of the things we'd been exploring at our church so that his community would see that he wasn't the only one thinking this way. I'm pretty sure he regrets that decision to this day.

He said I could speak about anything I wanted. He hoped it would be encouraging and stretching for his people. I hoped so too.

I had been doing quite a bit of thinking about the story of the Christian faith and how it had changed since the first century. I had been exploring the narrative of the life of the early followers of Jesus in the New Testament book of Acts, learning about how they arranged their lives in the first years of the church. And it seemed to me there was a lot in this story that the people at my friend's church could appreciate in light of their situation.

The Acts story introduces us to a man who was a staunch protector of the Jewish faith and was under orders to put an end to this sect of Jesus followers, at the time called "The Way." His name was Saul. He was infiltrating, persecuting, and destroying the upstart communities who declared Jesus as the fulfillment of the prophecies of the promised faith of Abraham. Saul was convinced that these people were deluded Jews who were weakening Judaism. He was trained as a Pharisee and believed that the Hebrew people were in such distress because of disobedience and wrong belief. He believed that if they would live in obedience to the Law of Moses, the blessing of God would return, and the Jews would be able to overcome the Roman-Gentile oppression.

I thought the story would fit really well with the life of this new church. Not only could the people connect with the story of the followers of Jesus experiencing the hope and trials of a burgeoning community, but I hoped they would see a correlation between Saul's story and their own.

Saul was a man of deep faith and conviction who was persecuting the new movement because it seemed to abandon what he believed to be the true, faithful way. Saul was not trying to kill the things of God; he was trying to keep them alive. But we know that he was literally killing what God was doing—and the people who were doing it.

I hoped the people would recognize that in the earliest days of Christianity—just as it is now—people who were motivated by the certainty of their belief assumed that they were perfecting life with God when in actuality they were blocking fresh expressions of what God was doing. I hoped they would see that even when we question the conclusions of others, we can do so without questioning their faithfulness. I hoped that by telling the story of the faithful but misguided attempts of Saul, I could encourage the people to be more patient, more grace-filled, and more open to those who held to a different version of the Christian story.

The story of Saul the persecutor takes a dramatic turn when he becomes a follower of the very Jesus he was seeking to stop and adopts the name Paul. I thought that this could be an encouragement to my friend and those in the church who were supportive of his ministry ideas. I hoped that they would find great encouragement in the story of someone who became fully embedded in the faith he had once sought to destroy. I believed that people would be buoyed by the idea that all is not lost when people opposed them, that there is always the hope of a Saul turning into a Paul.

So, I told them the Acts story, from the early church to Paul's leadership and travels. At one point Paul is arrested for proclaiming his newly understood faith and put under house arrest. The book of Acts ends with this rather abrupt summation: "For two whole years Paul stayed there in his own rented house and welcomed all who came to see him. He proclaimed the kingdom of God and taught about the Lord Jesus Christ—with all boldness and without hindrance!"[1] This was the real heart of my sermon. To me, it has important but easily missed implications for Christianity. It seems as though there was something meaningful for Paul, and for the other apostles, in the wording used in this section—Paul "proclaimed the kingdom of God and taught about the Lord Jesus Christ."

I suggested to the congregation that the early church had an understanding of the gospel that included two equally important elements: The first was teaching about Jesus—who he was, what he did, and what he taught. The second was preaching the kingdom of God and how Jesus engaged in it and invited others to do the same.

I tried to make the point that the early church was focused not solely on Jesus as a teacher but also on his role in bringing about the kingdom of God. I suggested that over time, the Christian story has tended to collapse the two ideas into one, with the kingdom of God part getting absorbed by the Jesus part. I suggested that many of us had become people who teach and preach only about Jesus and who, frankly, say almost nothing about the kingdom of God. I said that some of us had gone to church for decades and heard hundreds of sermons, studied hundreds of Sunday school lessons, and sung hundreds of songs about Jesus but rarely heard anything about the kingdom of God. I wondered aloud why this was the case.

I asked if we had perhaps become a faith hopping on one leg–teaching about Jesus–rather than a two-legged faith running on the teachings of Jesus *and* the proclamation of the kingdom of God.

I asked if we had perhaps become a faith hopping on one leg—teaching about Jesus—rather than a two-legged faith running on the teachings of Jesus *and* the proclamation of the kingdom of God.

I was really hitting my sermon stride here, if I do say so myself. I was driving home the idea that we needed to spend the same time, energy, thought, and creativity living the kingdom of God as we'd used to teach about Jesus. I said, "Maybe we have had too much Jesus at the expense of the kingdom of God."

At this point a man in the back, who, I'd noticed, wasn't quite digging what I was saying all along, finally had enough. He stood up and yelled, "No sir! No sir! No sir!" and walked out with a flourish. His protest gave others permission to express their dissatisfaction with what I was saying. People started speaking out, speaking at me. Compared to their normal sedate setting, this was pandemonium! I glanced over at my friend and saw a look of horror on his face as his head sunk low.

I felt terrible. I wasn't trying to make people mad or rattle them. I had hoped for dialogue, but I didn't intend for them to feel like they needed to shout down the preacher. I was a guest in their community, and it was never my intention—or my place—to cause them distress. I had wanted to give them permission to rethink their assumptions about the faith, to help them find that little kernel of hope that had been abandoned, blow the dust off of it, and say, "Remember how beautiful this is?" I know full well that nothing good happens when an outsider comes into a community and starts poking around and critiquing everything and disturbing the peace. It's like someone riding in my car and changing the presets on my stereo. And I had definitely changed their presets.

After the service, I stood by the door like a good pastor and waited to greet people, thinking I might be able to salvage some goodwill. Two people came up to me and said quietly, "You said what I've wanted to say for some time now, and

I thought it was right on." But everyone else looked at me like the drunken brother-in-law who belched at the table and insulted Grandma's famous meatloaf. For Minnesotans, who will muster up a "That was great, thanks for coming, please come again" for a plumber billing at double time, to walk past me with minimal eye contact and the occasional snort of disappointment was a sure sign that I had failed utterly.

The thing is, I believe in what I said. It can be disquieting for Christians to consider the possibility that we've been missing something in our faith, mainly because so many Christians approach faith with a zero-sum mentality. If something is added, something else must be taken away; there's not much room for tempering or balancing or expanding. So the suggestion that we have too much Jesus and not enough kingdom of God is threatening. It can sound like we need to get rid of Jesus altogether.

Still, it seems to me that too many of us have become Jesus-only and Jesus-always people and missed out on the fuller picture of what Jesus was about. Our tendency to focus on Jesus as the Christ and Savior has reshaped our understanding of the kingdom of God so dramatically that even the words we use to talk about the kingdom are loaded with meanings and concepts that have little to do with what Jesus or Paul meant when they used the phrase.

For most of my Christian life, I was taught that the kingdom of God is another way of talking about the afterlife and the world God will usher in when Christ returns for his final victory. Many of those in my Christian circle used "kingdom of heaven," the phrase Matthew used in his gospel, more often than "kingdom of God," which was favored by Mark and Luke. The word *heaven* gave the kingdom concept the sense of another time and another place. It certainly wasn't here on earth, where corruption and greed and evil ruled.

Jesus, we were told, was important primarily because he came to save us from our sins and help us get into God's heavenly kingdom someday. The Christian life was a kind of holding pattern in which we were stuck until God called us in for a landing at our real home. Or maybe we were being ejected from the fiery crash. I could never quite tell. Either way, the kingdom of heaven was something we had access to after death because Jesus' death and resurrection made it so. This was what Jesus was all about—giving us the key to our salvation, which would come to pass when we entered the gates of the kingdom of heaven.

Over time, however, I've come to believe that this kind of afterlife-dominant Christianity is not only a departure from the biblical story but might actually work against the very point of the Jesus agenda. The way I see it, Jesus was proclaiming something other than a faith of another time and another place. He was not suggesting a competition between here and there, between now and then. No, Jesus was proclaiming a holistic reorganization of all that is and all that will be. He was bringing about a new kind of life that was meant to be lived out right away, right here, and forevermore.

Jesus' message wasn't centered on individual people leaving this world and living in little rooms of glory in heaven. It was about the kingdom of God thriving on earth, just as it was in heaven. And this heaven was not another place but any place where God's agenda was fulfilled. The thrust of Jesus' life, of Jesus' teaching, of Jesus' preaching, of Jesus' miracles, was that

God is working in and through creation to bring all things into wholeness. Even if we misunderstand every other aspect of faith, we need to get this part right.

But we often don't, and that can have serious consequences. I remember hearing the question "Are you sure you're going to heaven?" at countless Christian crusades and youth rallies. It was usually phrased in a way that was meant to scare the listener into some serious soul-searching: "If you died tonight, would you wake up with Jesus?" or "If you died right now, where would you spend eternity?" or "If you died right now and God asked you why you should be let into heaven, what would you say?"

I know that the people asking these questions usually have the best of intentions. They are most likely doing all they can to share the good news as they understand it and to compel people to take it seriously. And there are people who have real and substantial questions about what happens after we take our final breath. But the way we ask the question sets the direction of the conversation. It reminds me of a prank question my dad used to ask his friends in public. He'd say, "So, Woody, do you still steal stuff from work?" My dad knew that there was no good way to answer this question, which is why he loved to tease his friends with it.

The heaven question functions the same way. It seems like a legitimate question, and many streams of Christian thought have thrived providing the answer to it. But it's a question that's almost impossible to answer. "Do you know where you will go?" has this limited sense to it. It clearly implies that there is a place. Embedded in the question is the expectation of a location called heaven as opposed to a location called hell. So to answer the question, one has to build a congruent view of these places called heaven and hell, of life and death, of God and faith and works. The question assumes an entire worldview.

What's troubling is that the worldview and cosmology and theology assumed in the question are culturally specific in their logic. For those of us living in a culture where present actions are evaluated by their future consequences, it might make sense to talk about where we will live in the great someday. But when missionaries in Papua New Guinea, for example, try to ask this question, they find that it's meaningless in a culture that has no concept of time or the future. Instead, that cultural narrative is based on the past, on what has already happened. They just don't have the language or the conceptual tools to think about the future the way we do. It doesn't make sense to them.

The same would have been true for Jesus. The Hebrew culture is also one that uses the past to talk about the present. It's quite different from the future-based worldview we have in Western Christianity. So if someone were to have asked Jesus an afterlife kind of question, I'm not sure he would have a satisfactory answer, at least not for anyone looking for an answer grounded in time and space. My guess is that he would say what he said when Thomas asked him where he was going: "I am the way and the truth and the life. No one comes to the Father except through me. If you really know me, you will know my Father as well. From now on, you do know him and have seen him."[2]

Jesus made it clear that the afterlife isn't a place. It's a state of being. It's the state in which all of God's hopes for the earth, all of God's desires for this partnership with humanity, come to fruition. The kingdom of God is made real in Jesus, the Messiah and Savior. The kingdom isn't somewhere else, waiting for us to die before we can be part of it. It is in us, through us, and for us right here, right now.

While it might not seem like it at first glance, even Jesus' comments about "going to prepare a place for you" and "in my Father's house there are many rooms" come from the rabbinic tradition and are meant to create a picture of God's redemption on earth. That's the way Jesus intended it and the way the disciples heard it.

When a Greek thinker heard this, he imagined going to the perfect places where the gods lived, in the heavens that existed

The kingdom isn't somewhere else, waiting for us to die before we can be part of it. It is in us, through us, and for us right here, right now.

apart from the earth. A Hebrew would also have thought of the place God lives but would have seen that place as existing in the midst of creation.

We've missed this sense of the kingdom as a present reality in part because of the term itself. I know it's the wording Jesus used, but sometimes words that had tremendous meaning in the time of Jesus have very little meaning for people like me. I live in the United States, where we haven't had a king in more than two hundred years. The same is true in countries all over the world. Even places that have active royalty rarely think of themselves as kingdoms anymore.

When Jesus used the term *kingdom of God,* it had a timely, lively, this-world sensibility. But when I hear it, it has none of that. I have to conjure up a picture of kings and subjects and thrones and princes and chariots. It pushes me into a world of fictitious monarchies, of Middle Earth and magical lands. It certainly doesn't have the deep meaning it ought to have when we're talking about joining with God in the healing of our everyday world.

For Jesus and his followers, however, the term was rich with revolution. The Jews were a minority class under the rule of Rome, and Rome had a very powerful king, Caesar. Well, to be clear, Caesar bore little resemblance to what we would think of as a king; Caesar declared himself a god. In fact, he declared that he should be referred to as "the Son of God." The places in his territory where he was honored as a god were referred to as *ekklesia,* the Greek word that was later used by Christians to refer to the church. So around the empire there were these communities that declared the kingdom of Caesar, the Son of God, and met in ecclesia for that purpose.

When Jesus declared that the kingdom of God was at hand, it sat in direct contrast to the kingdom of Caesar. It was a political call of how people ought to live in the midst of their world. When the followers of Jesus declared him to be the Son of God, they were doing so in contrast to the claims of the followers of Caesar. This was revolutionary language, and the only way it was allowed to stand was that the Jews had a tenuous agreement with the Romans: The Jews would not revolt against the power of Rome if they were allowed to worship their true God, Yahweh, and not Caesar. This was accomplished through high-level meetings with the Jewish ruling council and the local Roman rulers. Their agreement comes into play during the arrest and crucifixion of Jesus when the high priests converse with the Roman magistrate,

Pontius Pilate. So to belong to the kingdom of God was the alternative to belonging to the kingdom of Caesar. This had poignant and dangerous implications.

There was a revolutionary religious significance to this language as well. Remember that many Jews believed that the kingdom of Caesar would one day be replaced by the kingdom of David—in other words, they hoped they would be ruled by a Jew again. The Jewish story included the hope that the promised Messiah would bring about this shift in power. For many Jews, this hope was borne out by the existence of the Temple. It was built during David's reign and completed during the reign of his son Solomon. The Jews believed that the Messiah, the one in the line of David, would take up residence in the Temple again and reign as king. But Jesus declared that he was there to bring about the kingdom of God, not the kingdom of David, and that all people, Gentiles and Jews, were called to it.

Jesus stepped it up by suggesting that God would not reign in the Temple but rather in all who worship in spirit and in truth. That language set him in contrast with a segment of the Jewish people who believed that victory would come through the exertion of power, not love. This helps explain why some of the religious leaders of the day unexpectedly cooperated with the Romans in the execution of Jesus. His message of kingdom was threatening to both regimes in real-world ways.

In A.D. 70, when a revolt of Jewish rebels against Rome brought years of hatred and animosity to a boil, Caesar had the Temple destroyed. (It has never been rebuilt, a fact that still has great power in the Jewish story, as many Jews look forward to the day when it is rebuilt in Jerusalem.) That means that the Christians living in the post-Temple period knew that the life Jesus talked about was not centered in the Temple or in the churches of Caesar. They understood that their bodies were the temples and their communities were the churches. So when Paul preached about Jesus and proclaimed the radical, this-world message of the kingdom of God, they got it.

At the heart of Jesus' kingdom language is the idea that God is at work in the world and that we are invited to enter into that work. The kingdom-of-God gospel of Jesus calls us to partner with God, to be full participants in the life God is creating, to follow in the way of Jesus as we seek to live as people who are fully integrated with our Creator.

> **The kingdom-of-God gospel of Jesus calls us to partner with God, to be full participants in the life God is creating, to follow in the way of Jesus as we seek to live as people who are fully integrated with our Creator.**

As hopeful as all of this is, I know it leaves some nagging questions for those of us who were taught that heaven is a place with lots of joy and peace and singing, a place where our dead loved ones are waiting for us. To be honest, I don't have answers for all those questions.

I wish I did. Just the other day, I got one of those phone calls that comes from out of the blue and reminds us of the cruelty that accompanies the glories of life. It was from a friend who had been part of our church a number of years ago and had since gotten married and moved away. I was thrilled to hear her voice.

"Well, hello, Sarah! What's going on?"

"A lot, actually."

I knew from her tone that this was not going to be a happy conversation.

She said, "The last twelve days have been horrible. I was pregnant again and delivered our son Evan twelve days ago at twenty-four weeks." She went on to tell me that her baby had been doing really well but that he had developed an infection the day before and died during the night.

Tears immediately welled up in my eyes. Sarah's voice began to shake as she asked, "Could you come and help us figure out a funeral or something?" We made plans to meet at the funeral home in an hour to work out details. As I hung up the phone, I tried to prepare myself for the horrible pain I was about to enter into.

When we met, Sarah and her husband filled me in on the rest of the story. They were in the process of moving from Alaska to Florida and had stopped in Minnesota to visit family for a few weeks. That's when Evan was born far too soon. They went on to say what a miracle it was that they were with family and friends when all of this was happening, that they felt loved and cared for in the midst of their tragedy.

As we talked, I asked about their older son, who was about four. Sarah's husband, Jack, said, "Well, it's kind of hard for him to get his head around all of it. So I tried to explain it to him by saying that Evan was 'in the sky,' because heaven is just so hard for a child to understand." Jack paused and then continued, a certain rawness in his voice, "Now he keeps saying, 'Mom and Dad, I am going to go get baby Evan back from the sky and have him be here with us.'"

Sarah and Jack choked on their tears as Sarah said, "It is so good to have his sweet little voice and perspective in these hard days. He doesn't really know what's going on but says it best sometimes."

What Sarah and Jack and every one of us who have lost someone precious know is that the idea of heaven as a place isn't really the point. We talk about heaven as a physical location because it's one of the only ways we know how to express the good news

Being a person of faith means telling the story of hope, even when we don't have the words or capacity to understand how that hope is playing out.

of life winning out over death. We know we're not describing some metaphysical reality but rather expressing a hope, a belief, that God is present with those who have died, that one day God will heal the pain of death with the glory of reunion. For being a person of faith means telling the story of hope, even when we don't have the words or capacity to understand how that hope is playing out.

So when I talk in this chapter about the importance of having a full understanding of what Jesus meant when speaking about the kingdom of heaven, I know this idea is a bit removed from the reality of life for suffering parents. But I also know that when I talk about heaven as a place, that telling is a bit removed from the ultimate reality as well.

Because our questions about the afterlife have risen out of the Greek worldview, rather than the Hebrew culture of the early church, it's not surprising that we can find very little in the way of answers. But if we are willing to suspend the need for answers to those questions for a bit, I believe we find a whole other set of questions that are worth pursuing with equal passion.

The early Christians saw heaven not as a place we go to but as a reality that comes to us. They talked about redemption and healing coming through God's creation, not apart from it. They believed we would live as freed bodies in this healed place, not as freed spirits in some other place. Here is a section from the letter from Paul to the Romans that shows this sense:

> I consider that our present sufferings are not worth comparing with the glory that will be revealed in us. The creation waits in eager expectation for the children of God to be revealed. For the creation was subjected to frustration, not by its own choice, but by the will of the one who subjected it, in hope that the creation itself will be liberated from its bondage to decay and brought into the freedom and glory of the children of God.
>
> We know that the whole creation has been groaning as in the pains of childbirth right up to the present time. Not only so, but we ourselves, who have the first fruits of the Spirit, groan inwardly as we wait eagerly for our adoption, the redemption of our bodies.[3]

This is what we see in the Lord's Prayer: "Your kingdom come, your will be done on earth as it is in heaven."[4] Jesus and Paul continually try to inspire Christians to concern themselves with the here and now, to care for each other, to tend to the poor, to heal the sick, to love their enemies. They didn't speak of these as a way of killing time. This was it. And because all of creation is in a constant state of interaction and becoming, there is more goodness to come. This was the kingdom come to life on earth. This was what it meant to live with God here, now, and forevermore.

It's helpful to look at the way the book of Revelation articulates this view. John, who was writing about a dream he had, said:

> Then I saw "a new heaven and a new earth," for the first heaven and the first earth had passed away, and there was no longer any sea. I saw the Holy City, the new Jerusalem, coming down out of heaven from God, prepared as a bride beautifully dressed for her husband. And I heard a loud voice from the throne saying, "Look! God's dwelling place is now among the people, and he will dwell with them. They will be his people, and God himself will be with them and be their God. 'He will wipe every tear from their eyes.' There will be no more death or mourning or crying or pain, for the old order of things has passed away."[5]

The language of this book is intentionally cryptic, poetic, and imaginative. But it harks back to the words of the prophet Isaiah, who connected the "new heaven and new earth" to the promised Messiah and the fulfillment of God's agenda. There are places in Revelation where John is incredibly difficult to understand, but to me this passage is clear: this new heaven and new earth will be here, among the people, not somewhere else. The good news is that God will dwell among us, that God will be with us, that the whole of creation will be healed and restored and fully aligned with God. The kingdom of

God doesn't exist apart from earthly life. Earthly life will be made new as it is transformed into the kingdom of God.

It's fascinating to me that this ancient prophecy of a new heaven and new earth actually fits quite beautifully with the way scientists think about the universe. One of my favorite radio shows is *Speaking of Faith* on National Public Radio. My friend Krista Tippet wanted to create a place where people could come together to talk about issues of religion, meaning, and ethics, and this show is the very popular result of her dream. On March 8, 2007, the topic was Einstein's contribution to contemporary thought on creation and religion. I was particularly struck by Krista's introduction. She began:

> One of my guests today, the astrobiologist Paul Davies, offers this analogy: Until Einstein, people thought of time and space as fixed, unchanging and absolute, the backdrop to the great show of life. Einstein revealed that time and space themselves are elastic and mutable, that they exist in relationship with unfolding life. They are part of the show themselves. Time, space, matter, gravity, and light are all intertwined. They curve and collapse and change in response to each other. Such insights gave rise to the grand ideas that occupy physicists and cosmologists today: the big bang, black holes, quantum mechanics.

And, I would add, they can inspire grand ideas about heaven. It seems that every day brings about new ideas on life, death, the spirit, and the material world. The more I hear, the more I am convinced this is what Paul meant when he said, "For now we see only a reflection as in a mirror; then we shall see face to face. Now I know in part; then I shall know fully, even as I am fully known."[6] Our views, however developed they may be, are still only a glimpse of what God intended for us.

Yet this is still good news. We are not living in a stagnant universe, in a settled world where we have no choice but to wait for our departure to some other place where the rules are different. No, we are living in the midst of God's dynamic creation, filled with constant birthing, dying, and remaking. The cosmos is created with an openness to interplay. But this is not an unguided interplay; God is deeply embedded in it, driving it, guiding it to move and change and become more.

Salvation, rescue, release, healing—they come through the God who created all things, the God who is alive and involved in all things, the God who is actively remaking all things. They come when we participate in a living, dynamic relationship with God and one another, here, now, and forevermore.

> Salvation, rescue, release, healing—they come through the God who created all things, the God who is alive and involved in all things, the God who is actively remaking all things.

For me, this shift in my understanding of the kingdom of God being a removed, someday place to a belief that the kingdom come is the gospel message has had a dramatic impact on the way I see myself and the world around me. It's been a codebreaker for my reading of the Bible, making the Old and New Testaments fit together and make sense in ways they never did before. It's created a framework in which all these ideas about holism, the integrated God, and humanity as co-re-creators with God flow into a glorious worldview of hope and promise and possibility.

I feel like I have finally entered into the life with God I longed for as a young boy, the life where God and I are together all the time doing good work in the world. The story of heaven and salvation is not just wishful thinking. It is based in the reality of the world in which we live, the world that God is renewing every day and will continue to renew for all eternity. This is truly a faith of the past, present, and future. It is truly a Christianity worth believing.

NOTES

All biblical quotations are from *Today's New International Version (TNIV Bible)* (Grand Rapids, Mich.: Zondervan, 2005).

Chapter 4: The Wild Goose Chase

1 John 20:31
2 Father Vincent J. Donovan, *Christianity Rediscovered* (Maryknoll, N.Y.: Orbis Books, 2005), p. 148

Chapter 5: When Different Was Good

1 Acts 15:19
2 Acts 15:23–29
3 Justin Martyr, "The First Apology of Justin," ch. 20; Justin Martyr, "The Second Apology of Justin for the Christians, Addressed to the Roman Senate" ch. 13; earlychristianwritings.com

Chapter 6: It's in the Way That You Use It

1 Ephesians 6:13–17

2 Ephesians 6:12

3 2 Timothy 3:16

4 2 Timothy 3:10–17

Chapter 8: Together, Again

1 Matthew 22:37

2 Mark 12:30

3 Luke 10:27

4 Colossians 3:11

5 John 14:19–20

Chapter 9: Up and Out

1 "The Westminster Confession of Faith" (1646), ch. 3, paras. 1–5, www.reformed.org/documents/index.html

Chapter 10: Down and In

1 Deuteronomy 32:11

2 1 Thessalonians 2:7

3 Matthew 23:37

Chapter 11: Wonderfully Made

1 "The Westminster Confession of Faith" (1646), ch. 6, www.reformed.org/documents/wcf_with_proofs

2 "Augsburg Confession" (1530), in Theodore G. Tappert, *The Book of Concord: The Confessions of the Evangelical Lutheran Church* (Philadelphia: Augsburg/Fortress, 1959), p. 29

3 *Book of Common Prayer* (1928), justus.anglican.org/resources/bcp/1928/Articles_Religion.pdf

4 Franklin Graham, quoted in Cathy Lynn Grossman, "Billy Graham's Son Takes the Pulpit, His Own Way," *USA Today,*

Mar. 7, 2006, www.usatoday.com/news/nation/2006-03-07-franklin-graham-cover_x.htm

Chapter 12: Same as It Ever Was

1 Genesis 1:26–28
2 Genesis 2:25
3 Genesis 2:15–17
4 Genesis 3:1–11
5 Matthew 5:43–48
6 Ezekiel 18:23
7 Ezekiel 18:32
8 John 3:17
9 1 Timothy 4:10
10 2 Peter 3:9

Chapter 13: There Goes the Judge

1 Mark 2:27–28
2 Matthew 5:38–42
3 Matthew 5:43–48
4 Dallas Willard, *The Divine Conspiracy: Rediscovering Our Hidden Life in God* (New York: HarperCollins, 1998)
5 Matthew 21:28–32
6 Romans 1:20

Chapter 14: Behind Blue Eyes

1 Psalm 103:11–13
2 "The Numbers Count: Mental Disorders in America," www.nimh.nih.gov/publicat/numbers.cfm

Chapter 15: The Jew I Never Knew

1 See Matthew 1:20–22
2 Matthew 5:17

Chapter 16: You Say You Want a Revolution

1 Genesis 15

2 See Acts 10

3 Matthew 26:52

4 Luke 4:15–20

5 Isaiah 9: 1–7

Chapter 17: I Didn't Know Him from Adam

1 Luke 1:26–38

2 Luke 2:34–35

3 Matthew 8:26

4 Colossians 1:9

5 "The Nicene Creed" (A.D. 325), www.reformed.org/documents/index.html

6 "The Westminster Confession of Faith" (1646), ch. 8, para 2, www.reformed.org/documents/index.html

7 "The Definition of the Council of Chalcedon" (A.D. 451), www.reformed.org/documents/index.html

8 John 14:12

9 Romans 4:18–5:19

10 John 14:1–31

Chapter 18: Heaven on Earth

1 Acts 28:30–31

2 John 14:6–7

3 Romans 8:18–23

4 Matthew 6:10

5 Revelation 21:1–4

6 1 Corinthians 13:12

ACKNOWLEDGMENTS

The making of this book has been a long journey. In one sense I have been writing this book my entire life, but more specifically, it has been nearly three years in coming. In that time the book has had numerous configurations and countless titles. It started in a conversation with my friend John Raymond, who suggested that I lay out the hope-filled version of invitational Christianity I always talk about by telling my own personal story. This took some convincing, and I am so thankful to him for the idea and encouragement.

From the start *A Christianity Worth Believing* was a communal creation. There are so many people without whom this book would not have been possible, from those who loved me into faith in my teenage years to the friendly (and at times not so friendly) critics who have pushed me to think clearly and act kindly to the people of Solomon's Porch, my local community of faith, and the people of Emergent Village, my extended community of faith.

Above all, I was buoyed in this process by the most important person in my life, my best friend and wife, Shelley. While writing, I often become crabby and single-minded, and Shelley is forced to live—literally—with the consequences of the process.

I am indebted to my professional partners in this effort: Sheryl Fullerton, my editor at Jossey-Bass; Kathy Helmers, my agent; and Carla Barnhill, my editor, friend, and writing coach. It is not possible to overstate the importance of Carla in this book and in my being an author. Carla was a brilliant, insightful, and committed partner in the creation of this book.

I am also grateful for the insights of Mike Stavlund, Tony Jones, Michael Toy, Scot McNight, and Facebook friends who made the book better with their input, reflections, and comments.

Thank you to all who have given so graciously in helping to make *A Christianity Worth Believing* possible.

D. P.

THE AUTHOR

Doug Pagitt is a social and theological entrepreneur. He is the founder of Solomon's Porch, a holistic missional Christian community in Minneapolis, Minnesota (www.SolomonsPorch.com), and is one of the founders of Emergent Village, a social network of Christians leaders around the world (www.EmergentVillage.com).

Doug and his wife, Shelley, have been married for twenty years and are the parents of four teenagers.

Doug holds a degree in anthropology from Bethel University and a master of arts degree in theology from Bethel Seminary. He has worked in churches and for a nonprofit foundation and owns three businesses in Minneapolis.

Doug is a sought-after speaker and consultant for churches, denominations, and businesses throughout the United States and around the world on issues of postmodern culture, social systems, and Christianity.

He is the author, editor, and coeditor of many books, including *Church Re-Imagined* (Zondervan, 2004), *Preaching Re-Imagined* (Zondervan, 2005), *BodyPrayer* (Waterbrook, 2005), and *An Emergent Manifesto of Hope* (Baker Book House, 2007).

Doug can be reached through his Web site, www.DougPagitt.com.